Nobody's Baby Now

Nobody's Baby Now

REINVENTING YOUR ADULT

RELATIONSHIP WITH YOUR

MOTHER AND FATHER

Susan Newman, Ph.D.

WALKER & COMPANY
NEW YORK

In memory of my parents,

Anita and Irving

Copyright © 2003 by Susan Newman

All rights reserved. No part of this book may be reproduced or transmitted in any form or by any means, electronic or mechanical, including photocopying, recording, or by any information storage and retrieval system, without permission in writing from the Publisher.

First published in the United States of America in 2003 by Walker Publishing Company, Inc.

Published simultaneously in Canada by Fitzhenry and Whiteside, Markham, Ontario L3R 4T8

For information about permission to reproduce selections from this book, write to Permissions, Walker & Company, 435 Hudson Street, New York, New York 10014

Library of Congress Cataloging-in-Publication Data
Newman, Susan
Nobody's baby now : reinventing your adult relationship with your mother and father / Susan Newman
p.   cm.
Includes index.
ISBN 0-8027-1407-2 (alk. paper)
1. Parent and adult child.   2. Adult children—Family relationships.   3. Adult children—Attitudes.   I. Title.

HQ755.86.N489   2003
306.874—dc21   2003043254

Book design by Jennifer Ann Daddio

Visit Walker & Company's Web site at www.walkerbooks.com

Printed in the United States of America
2   4   6   8   10   9   7   5   3   1

Contents

Preface   ix
Acknowledgments   xv

Introduction   1
    Necessary Alterations   2
    My Parent, My Friend   4

One: Who Am I? Who Are They?   7
    The Family Fishnet   9
    Different Generations, Different Views   11
    Your History Together   17
    Making Choices, Initiating Change   18
    Still Your Parents   22

Two: Still Driving You Crazy   25
    So Annoying   27
    Addressing Trouble Spots   36
    Coping with Relationship Gaps   43
    Your New, Leading Role   51

Three: Staying Connected   53

    Short-Circuiting Guilt Trips   55

    The Frequency Factor   58

    The Near or Far Dilemma   61

    Turning Estranged Relationships Around   63

    Keeping Everyone Happy   66

Four: Drawing Boundaries   71

    Defining Boundaries   74

    Changing Patterns   76

    Who's the Parent?   80

Five: Your Partners, Spouses, and In-Laws   87

    I'd Like You to Meet . . .   89

    The Underlying Issues   90

    Surmounting In-Law Difficulties   96

Six: Your Parent's New Partner   101

    Puzzling Choices   102

    New Families, New Roles   106

    Unraveling the Logistics   111

    Seeing Things Differently   114

Seven: Sibling Complications,
Sibling Support   117

    The Family System   118

    Sibling Frustrations   120

    Troublemakers and High-Maintenance Siblings   121

    You Like Him Better . . . Still   125

    Sibling Assistance   129

Eight: Money Matters   133
   Receiving Money from Your Parents   136
   Claiming Rights to Your Parents' Money   141
   When Parents' Generosity Makes You
      Uncomfortable   145
   Parents Needing Financial Help from You   148

Nine: Career Directions and Decisions   154
   Great Expectations   156
   Going into the Family Business   158
   Measuring Up   163
   Surpassing a Parent   165

Ten: Relationship Shifts   169
   Illness Changes the Relationship   170
   When a Parent Dies   173
   Losing Your Childhood Home   175

*Eleven: It's a Boy! Parents as
Grandparents*   178
   Not Living Up to Your Expectations   181
   Expectations Met   184
   Inevitable In-Law Comparisons and Conflicts   186
   Protecting Your Own   190

*Twelve: Parent to Peer—The
Friendship Model*   197
   Starting Points   199
   Eight Ground Rules for Ensuring Friendship   202
   The Intangibles That Fortify Friendships   217

Thirteen: A Work in Progress—
The Generational Picture   219
   From the Same Cloth   220
   Parents Are People, Too   222
   And the Bond Goes On . . .   225
   Modeling for the Next Generation   226

Author's Note   229
Index   232

Preface

As a child, your relationship with your parents was relatively straightforward: You were told what to do and how to do it, and for the most part, you did it. Now that you are a grown-up, the relationship is far more layered and complex because you have clear options, many more than you may think, to direct the course of the relationship with even the most difficult parents.

Unfortunately, my mother and I had only a few years to interact as adult child and parent, to become friends, before she died. My father, on the other hand, lived a long time, but his death made me wonder if I had made the most of our relationship. After he died, I watched friends interact with their parents and noticed that when parents and adult children related more as peers, the relationships were richer and seemed to flourish; those in it were happier and genuinely enjoyed each other. In contrast, when the childhood regime with mother and father exerting their power remained installed, the likelihood of disagreement and estrangement rode near the surface, erupting far too frequently.

Why then doesn't every family have, or at least strive for, a more equitable balance of power once the children are grown up? And how do adults with a peer-peer bond with their parents achieve it? As a social psychologist, I was drawn to these questions, and they became the basis of a two-year research study. Almost all of the adult children-parent studies and books center on parents' points of view; those from the offsprings' points of view tend to look at subjects relating to caring for aging parents or coping with dysfunction resulting from alcoholism or abuse. It was time to find out what *adult children think* about relationships with their healthy, independent parents—what they hope for from the relationship, how they deal with their parents' shortcomings, and how they move the relationship in the direction they want it to go.

I interviewed adult children about their relationships with their parents and made note of when, why, and how these people faltered or triumphed, how they released themselves from unchanging, frustrating parent-child struggles. The 150 adults I interviewed formally were between the ages of twenty-seven and fifty-five, and the others I observed or talked to informally all had at least one living parent who was financially independent and living on his or her own. To protect everyone's privacy, all names and identifying characteristics have been changed. These men and women hold jobs that span a wide spectrum— from affluent attorneys and stockbrokers to graphic designers, physical therapists, and carpenters. Interestingly, it didn't matter what a person's socioeconomic level was— concerns about and issues with parents were strikingly similar. Similarities held among heterosexuals and homosexuals, single and married people, as well as among those with or without children.

From this broad picture it became clear that not only do your and your parents' histories—together and apart—play a key role in the relationship you have now, but also that sisters and brothers from the same family navigate the course in their own unique ways. I found adult children who operate—or angrily cooperate—with their parents as if they were still fifteen-year-olds, others who are parenting their parents too soon, and still others who dismiss their parents, though unwillingly—seemingly lost about how to rectify what they perceive to be untenable and irreparable situations.

You'll read intensely personal histories, and undoubtedly recognize a familiar parent type—an intrusive mother, a domineering or overprotective father, a parent who is uncommunicative or one who is too stubborn. You will witness familiar scenarios as well—holiday conflicts, sibling favoritism, manipulation through parental money, a lack of warmth and affection, a parent's need to be "right," and many, many more. You'll gain insight into the dynamics of your own family and make discoveries that may never have occurred to you, things that will clarify what you may not have understood about your parents. Personal accounts from adult children demonstrate how to take advantage of similar interests and how to meet on a new, neutral field, how to build on childhood experiences, and how to turn a thorny relationship into a fulfilling one.

Overwhelmingly, most adult children feel fully vested in their relationships with their parents and have a strong desire to enhance or get more out of the bond. From the lives of those who volunteered their stories, I culled simple everyday schemes, methods, and scenarios that worked for them, and that can show you how to overcome difficulties with your parents, circumvent most obstacles, and emulate the successes. You will gain understanding of your parents, acquire the confidence to know what you want from them, and be able to ask for it in much the same way you would approach and ask a friend. A clear model of friendship developed from the research, with many of the elements and tools people use to establish and maintain peer friendships. The Friendship Model, discussed in chapter 12, will be useful as you transform your parent into a peer.

In some instances, you'll discover a fresh approach to a tradition that has lost its momentum or a way to start anew. You may become alert to a situation you didn't think about or think important, but one that could make a huge difference in your relationship with your parents. What you will read is designed to help you capitalize on opportunities to be with or relate to your parents, to make them happy as they age, and to help you enjoy them from your adult point of view, whether your parents are quietly enjoying a slow-paced retirement or running marathons.

When talking to people about their parents, I was surprised by how much their stories focused on seizing opportunities, forging stronger bonds, and establishing positive parent-to-peer relationships, no matter how tumultuous the parent-to-child ties once were. It was obvious these people recognized that it's a two-way street—your wishes hold equal weight with those of your parents, and at times more. This is a dramatic shift in the dynamics of your relationship, and an invaluable one in helping you create a peer-to-peer bond with the people who raised you. Sharing in the stories of other adult children will also help you learn how to act on your wishes while building a friendship, one that goes far deeper than your parent-child attachment. If you also are the parent of an adult child, what you read will be doubly useful.

With periods of health greatly extended for the older population, you can expect to have your parents around longer, giving you the opportunity to reap the rewards of your markedly improved relationship. By adapting ideas and suggestions to your situation, you should be able to look back years or decades from now and say, "I did it right, I have no regrets. My parent was my friend."

Acknowledgments

Researchers and writers have ideas all the time that for the most part remain undeveloped unless others stand behind them. For their faith in this project and in my work, which allowed me to share my discoveries, I am grateful to agent Michael Carlisle, publisher George Gibson, and editor Jackie Johnson, who cared for and shaped my idea.

Almost every adult child has an opinion about relationships with parents. My close friends—they know who they are—are no exception. I welcomed and as always value their input and perspectives. Among them, and for his time and dedication to this book, I thank my husband, Richard, who never tired of adult child-parent conversations, who offered his insights, and who willingly read pages whenever I asked. Special thanks to Ruth Hague, who used her vast professional knowledge of family interaction to sort out the stickier issues and steer me in better directions; to Janet Spencer King, who read the manuscript in many different stages and provided invaluable guidance; and to Dilys Winn, who remained my ardent cheerleader and problem solver from the idea's inception to the book's completion.

However, *Nobody's Baby Now* would not exist without the people who enthusiastically and graciously talked to me, a stranger, about their lives and their parents. I appreciate their candor and for trusting me with their stories. And for helping me keep thousands of interview comments and details organized and for their many thoughtful contributions, thank you to Rachael Alvarez and Jessie Mishkin.

Introduction

A few years ago, while my father was chatting on about his favorite subject, the stock market (as if I cared), I did what I had always done when he talked about things I consider over my head: I drifted. My thoughts skipped from what's for dinner, to my son's grades, to a deadline I just might make if I wrote eleven chapters by Friday. Every so often, I'd catch a word or two—"NASDAQ," "split two for one"—and nod my head as if I were really listening, then drift back into my own world.

This scene played out too many times over several decades until my father finally became annoyed and said, "Susan, it's impossible to have a conversation with you when you're acting like a typical kid with a very short attention span."

Not only did he now have my full attention, but I also got the point. He was trying to connect with me adult to adult. I, on the other hand, was foiling him by acting like a teenager who routinely tunes out people, places, and things that won't affect her in the next ten minutes. At some point my father had made the transition from treating me as a child to treating me as an adult, but I had not moved from treating my father as a parent to treating him as a peer.

Whenever he tried to cultivate my interest in the stock market, I paid no attention. I missed a grand chance to be my father's appreciative student and to know him better. I knew him well, and our relationship was close, but looking back, I see it could have had yet another dimension. Had I listened, he would have been so pleased that I showed some interest in his passion, and I would have had a savvy portfolio.

Necessary Alterations

Rediscovering your parents and reducing conflict as an adult is forward movement of the most rewarding kind. You spent a good portion of your life attempting to become independent of your parents, to draw operational and emotional lines between you, and even though you've reached adulthood in other areas of your life, it's hard to let go of patterns ingrained during childhood and the teen years. Throughout most of the first two decades of your life you relied on your parents, maybe took them for granted at different points. But now that you're an adult, you're independent of them.

Independence can be defined geographically, by your marital status or living arrangement, by your age, or, perhaps most significantly, by your emotional bond. However, while the emotional bond formed in childhood and adolescence can sustain your relationship with your parents and lovingly guide it through your adult years, that connection can also keep you too tightly tied and dependent. Gaining your independence may require loosening the grip of that bond.

At times it may seem virtually impossible to alter the "dances" you've been doing with your parents for most of your life—those enduring, frequently difficult and damaging, time-warped behavior patterns. No matter what you think about your parents and your areas of disagreement, be they temporary glitches or long-standing problems, both you and your parents can benefit by making adjustments in how you relate to each other. You can develop a new perspective, reset your tolerance level, address different needs, and find better ways of coping with behaviors that still bother or hurt you.

Given today's medical advances and healthier lifestyles, most parents of adult children are capable and vital—ready to engage in ways their parents didn't or couldn't—and will need little assistance from their children for decades, if at all. You have the chance to turn your relationship into a flourishing one—neither stagnant nor bland and far less harmful or stressful than it has been. And it's likely you will have many years to savor the reward for the effort you make.

Regardless of the specifics of the relationship you have with your parents, *Nobody's Baby Now* is your guide for sustaining a good relationship, developing one if it was absent while you were growing up, and fixing those aspects that are less than ideal . . . for the long haul. You and your parent(s) may not agree on spouse choice (yours or theirs), attitudes toward work, who keeps house, or how you and your partner raise the children. But there are strategies you can use to minimize the strains and pulls and obvious conflict. Even if you believe your parents can't or won't change, there's room for alterations that will, if nothing else, ease tensions and build mutual tolerance for annoying situations. With resentments eased and tolerance levels raised, you'll become less susceptible to the things that upset you and more open to the satisfactions of a loving relationship with your parents.

My Parent, My Friend

The schism between you and your parents may be wider and deeper than the natural differences that existed during your teen years. Nonetheless, you can make a lot of the old, tangled interaction disappear with concerned involvement now that you yourself are an adult. My mother and I had a particularly stormy relationship during my adolescence, yet as adults, we transformed it through, of all things, the simple act of cooking. I was a classic example of the child, the teenager, the young adult, struggling to be free of her parents, of the incessant advice and parental worry. Once I became an adult, seeking my mother's advice changed how we related. I needed help, and she loved giving it. My mother became my personal Emeril Legasse. I called her on a regular basis to find out how she prepared her special crust for apple pie and what vinegar she used in her salad dressing. I had to know why my lemon pie ran and hers didn't. I relied on her for endless tidbits of information, from oven temperature to bake potatoes to how long to boil a corned beef and how often to change its water. She was my guru on what froze well and what didn't. Food questions formed our initial adult bond and quickly created a different path for relating.

Eventually, as my culinary skills advanced, she began to ask me how I made a particular dish. The years of tension and grief were forgotten. We became caring friends, equals who loved and respected each other. We laughed when a soufflé collapsed or when we concocted risky combinations to salvage a lackluster soup and served it to unsuspecting guests. We were partners, peers, in a harmless hoax to save her or my "entertaining" face. The more we shared, the closer we became in other areas of our relationship.

Establishing and accepting your role as an adult in your parents' lives will enable you to see your parents as people and to relate to them as adults, sharing information about what's going on in your and their lives. Parental advice may continue to play a role, but as the peer-peer bond matures, you are as likely to be making suggestions as your parent. As you move on with your independent life, the relationship will develop into one with a more balanced give-and-take.

The shift to a more equitable relationship is a process of putting aside anger and resentment for everyone; for some the process is a difficult journey. However, it is possible to pull an emotionally distant parent close and to distance an overly involved one without permanently hurting a parent's feelings or damaging your bond. You may need to change how *you* think about your parents and how you approach a problem involving them. The rewards for extracting the stressful undercurrent and difficulties that run beneath the surface of your relationship are many. Get-togethers will become less fraught with tension, less forced or mandated. Your time together will likely become enriched with more fun and humor. And most significantly, that time will be infused with a sense of peer-level camaraderie.

As parents age, they often become unable or less inclined to participate actively in their children's lives. When that happens, adult children, myself included, sadly consider what might have been and realize too late what they missed by settling for cordial, superficial relationships, or worse, by falling into angry, antagonistic patterns left over from the growing-up years. In these pages you'll find the tools to keep disagreements to a minimum, to turn intolerable situations around, and to harness potentially painful interactions or hold them at bay. A single gesture or a few words can create a bridge of understanding to your parents, whether they live around the corner or across the country. The effects reported by interviewees ranged from subtle to transforming; their experiences and observations have the potential to make a huge difference in your and your parents' lives as well.

The time you have with your parents is limited and precious; preferably you will spend it happily getting to know and understand them as friends. They are the people who fed you and brought you up, who guided you through the circuitous route to adulthood. You are who you are in large part because of them, and you have an opportunity to make a difference in your future relationship with them, to enjoy them as an adult, and to forge a relationship that only the best and most intimate of peers usually have.

ONE

Who Am I? Who Are They?

Before you can guide your adult child-parent relationship forward, you need to know where the relationship is and how it got there. What impedes the relationship? What sparks it? What keeps it vital—or stagnant?

Even if your parents are irksome, critical, or cranky, the bond you have with them has taken years to form and is far stronger and more resilient than any single annoying personality trait or difference of opinion. The sore point in your relationship may be your parents' attempts to control your life, or how you or they handle money. You may have a parent who overdoes the worrying or whose constant criticism makes you feel inferior. Some of your difficulties may not be with your parent per se, but with your parent's new partner. You may be having a hard time accepting and adjusting to this person in your parent's life. It's quite possible the time you spend with your parents feels like work.

The broader questions that follow will help you gauge the current relationship you have with your parents and

identify rocky and uncomfortable areas that need attention. By answering them in a careful, thoughtful way, you
will find a starting point and be ready to remedy the difficulties. For example, if you answer no to the first question—feeling you do most of the giving or provide most of
the support—you may want to consider being less available to your parents, but that is only one of the possibilities you will find for correcting that particular problem.

Perhaps you answer yes to the question about feeling
guilty when you hear your parent's voice. There's a fine
line between the sense of obligation that creates guilt and
the sense of connection that makes you want to stay in

PINPOINTING PROBLEM AREAS IN
RELATIONSHIPS WITH YOUR PARENTS

- Does the relationship feel balanced to you?
- Do you feel your parents expect too much from you?
- Are they too involved in your life? Too demanding of
  your time?
- Do they influence your thinking too much?
- Do you and they communicate too often? Too little?
- Are too many or not enough topics off-limits?
- Are boundaries clearly defined and understood?
- Can you talk to your parents about your feelings?
- Are your parents as affectionate as you would like
  them to be?
- Do they respect your feelings?
- Do you tense up or feel guilty when you hear your
  parent's voice?
- From your point of view, is the relationship gratify-
  ing?

---

touch or be with your parents. You will be able to replace the word "should" with "want to" or "look forward to" in regards to being with your parents when you replace feelings of obligation with choice. Friction lessens when *you choose* to share experiences as part of loving and caring, rather than from feelings of duty or responsibility.

As you respond to each question, make note of the areas you would like to improve—for example, have your parents less involved in your daily life, strive for a more loving and respectful relationship, reduce the tension between you, or find more shared interests. Your list will serve as a map to keep you focused as you discover solutions with which to tackle the troubling parts and to bring you much closer to where you want your answers—and the relationship—to be. You can form a friendship with your parents, no matter what the problems are and where you begin, if you address the practical and emotional issues that bother you.

Now, with a cursory reading of your relationship's strengths and weaknesses, you're ready to reassess the time you devote and your connection to your parents and learn how to keep them in your life without feeling overly stressed or annoyed. You'll also begin to acknowledge, if you haven't already, that you have priorities, too, that may take precedence over parents' requests. Without too much effort, you can be successful at keeping all the significant people in your life happy, including yourself.

The Family Fishnet

Even when you are an adult, your yearning for closeness with your parents and a desire to please them can create a strong dose of guilt when you can't meet your parents' expectations—to call, to spend Saturday with them, to be home for Thanksgiving, to be there whenever they may need you, to be successful in your career, to marry, to have children . . . and the list goes on and on. Parental pressures are much like a fishnet surrounding your entire life. How cramped the space feels to you depends on your emotional makeup, your feelings about your parents, and how tightly they wield the net.

Dorianne's parents hold a tight rein. They comment or offer advice on everything, from Dorianne's appearance to her and her husband's finances. "Both my parents are weight obsessed. They don't say anything if I gain weight, but if I lose a few pounds, they make a big deal about it. My mother is very conscious of what I wear. When I know I'm going to see her, I am definitely more conscious of how I dress."

Neither of Dorianne's parents entirely trusts her to handle personal or financial situations by herself. She told a friend at work a personal secret, and her mother asked her if she was sure the friend knew not to tell anyone. Dorianne objects. "Really! I'm thirty years old, and she's questioning my judgment. Same thing with my dad: When a piece of furniture was delivered damaged, he insisted the company give us a new table. We were fine with someone coming to repair the one we had, but my dad wasn't. When I was looking for a new job, he tried to tell me what to say to get a higher salary."

If you savor your independence, having a parent watch over your life or any aspect of it can feel prickly. Your parents, like Dorianne's, may try to exert across-the-board influence—from where you live and with whom you socialize to how you should dress for a job interview. On the other hand, you may feel slighted by your parents if they tend to be more hands-off. Thirty-four-year-old Jessica is angry because her mother is removed and seemingly uninterested in Jessica's life. "My dad always told us, 'You have to meet your mother halfway,'" she explains. "I've gone beyond halfway, but she's never reached the halfway mark. I have a mom who lives thirty minutes away from me. Do you think we've gone out to lunch? Not once. She's never asked me to go shopping. I've tried to include her, and she's really not interested. If she made the slightest effort, I'd jump at it. If she said, 'Jessica, come over, and we'll bake cookies for the children,' I'd be in shock, but I'd be in the car."

Kathrine, a thirty-one-year-old motivational speaker, is likewise frustrated by her mother's lackadaisical approach to hers and her brother's visits. When either of them fly in, rather than picking them up at the airport, their mother has them ride the airport bus because she prefers to use the hour to stay longer at her office or to catch up on phone calls at home. She doesn't see her refusal to come to the airport in a bad way or consider that her children's feelings might be hurt. Her daughter feels otherwise. "There are certain things I care about that I think are important to our relationship, and she just doesn't see them."

Different Generations, Different Views

Your parents' parenting tendencies hinge in large part on their personal history. Since you and your parents are from different generations, you have different expectations, mores, and attitudes; your opposing views can have a profound impact on the relationship. Even if you have a lot in common and agree on many issues, you may be miles apart on such important subjects as religion, sex, politics, and child rearing.

"My parents can't imagine that you can be friends with the opposite sex," says Will, who is forty-five and single. "You either date women or you marry them. You don't live with them platonically, and you certainly don't have sex if you're not married. My parents were dating during a time when the worst thing and greatest shame was to be unmarried and become pregnant."

A same-sex, different-religion, or ethnically mixed relationship may set off parental alarms, too. When midway through his teens, thirty-five-year-old Nicholas told his parents he was gay, his father thought his son was being brainwashed. Nicholas had to cope with a parent whose upbringing had taught him not to be proud of anyone gay. Similarly, Ryan, who is six years older than Nicholas, grew up in an even harsher era when openness about gay issues was an anomaly. "Then, being gay was considered a psychological error, and you would be sent to a shrink who tried to 'fix' you. Today kids and parents see gays on television, in the news, in plays and movies, in soap operas. That's not to say the acceptance is great today, but the odds are better coming out now then they were when I was a teenager. I haven't told them I'm gay. My parents would never understand," says Ryan.

Parents raised in the pretherapy generation can be uncomfortable and unreceptive to offspring who show their emotions and say what they think and feel. Sarah, thirty-seven, a product of years of therapy in an era of openness, deals with this aspect of the generation divide. Her mother is a Holocaust and divorce survivor, and Sarah sees her as very strong, but emotionally shut off. "She has a survivor mentality; her job in life is to take care of everyone else," notes Sarah. "She's always there when she's needed, but has no enthusiasm for life. I think she loves me and her grandchildren, but it's just a different kind of love—not the touchy-feely connection I would prefer."

The mere mention of therapy or counseling can be repellent to parents who consider it taboo. Christina sent Jim, her fiancé, ahead to her hometown to live with her mother and stepfather and house hunt while she finished up her job in another city. Jim and her mother were getting along fairly well until one evening, her mother told Jim that she has low self-esteem and is a martyr. Jim innocently said, "If you recognize this about yourself, you can change it. There is help out there."

"My mother interpreted his recommendation as 'You need mental help,' and was outraged. She stopped speaking to him. Therapy carries a huge stigma for her," explains Christina.

Many of your goals for yourself may also be different from your parents', another reflection of a different era. Lana, an unmarried twenty-eight-year-old communications executive, has a mother who simply can't understand where Lana is in her life. When her mother was twenty-eight, she was married, with two children and a husband who supported them. Her mother thinks Lana is not trying hard enough to meet a husband. The difference in outlook is a source of frustration in their relationship.

Although thirty-six-year-old Tina's mother grew up in the same generation as Lana's, they had very different goals for their daughters. For Tina's mother and other women raised in the '40s and '50s, marriage was commonly the only way to get out of their parents' house. Tina's mother had five children by the time she was twenty-eight. "In one sense she feels she squandered part of her life by having her children so early," says Tina. "She missed so many opportunities that she wants for her children, she doesn't talk to me about having children."

Generational differences aside, you should look at your parents' individual backgrounds—where they came from and how they got there. This can explain much about why they act as they do with you: People learn roles based on childhood experiences and continue to play them even if they no longer serve a purpose. The parent who was raised in poverty, whose parents struggled to feed the family, for instance, may have attitudes about money that on the surface seem odd or overzealous to someone who grew up in an age of relative prosperity. Michael explains how his parents' childhoods and attitudes affected his life. "My parents grew up in the depression, so I will always have a frugal side to me. I have overcompensated for my parent's concerns about education by getting a master's degree in sports psychology, partially because I thought that's what they wanted versus what I really wanted to do."

A parent may have insisted on your having a college education precisely because he didn't have one. Another parent may have insisted on that same education precisely because she did. A complex grouping of childhood experiences filters into how one parents. The father of Marcus, a forty-five-year-old African-American comptroller for a large corporation, grew up in the South and walked the color line every day of his life. "His childhood stories are a lifetime away from my experiences," remarks Marcus. "His self-image issues, feelings of rejection, and his anger made him difficult to live with. He was demanding of all his children, hoping we would be more accepted if we succeeded in school and in our jobs."

Thea, thirty-two and married, observes that her mother has always been overprotective of Thea and her sister, in part because she grew up dirt-poor and isolated in a small rural town. Her entire focus was on the kind of life she wanted for her children. She did whatever was necessary to care for Thea and her sister.

"My dad left when we were very young; being alone and poor put my mother on the thin edge of panic. She's afraid of large cities and freeways," Thea elaborates. "If I mention I have to travel to Los Angeles, Chicago, or New York, she gets hysterical. She's afraid I'm going to die, but her fears and protectiveness, as annoying as they are, make sense to me, given her childhood and very limited exposure beyond her tiny town."

Your parents may overcompensate for what they feel they lacked as children. Amy's father was an active and demanding parent because his own dad had not been. Her father was a late-in-life baby—his dad was in his sixties when he was born. He viewed his relationship with his dad as more like being raised by a grandfather, so he didn't have much of a role model to go by on how to be a father himself. "But rather than being an occasional parent like his father, my dad was very hands-on in my upbringing," says Amy.

How much you do or don't rely on your parents—or they on you—is often an indication of how your parents were reared. If, for example, your parents are products of close-knit families with midwestern values, who were raised when few questioned family togetherness and when many children stayed close to home, they may balk at your choice to live thousands of miles from home. Beyond the desire to lead a life independent of parents, opposing values and belief systems can cause major upheaval between you and your parents, particularly when divorce, religion, or social position are involved.

Delia, thirty-four, struggles with two of these issues at once—her marriage is falling apart, and she's a heavy drinker, both of which conflict with her parents' faith. The differences in how she and her parents lead their lives have created a wall, based in part on Delia's need to keep the truth from them. "I wish I could be more honest with them, but I don't in any way live like a Southern Baptist should. My parents don't believe in breaking up the family, and my drinking would distress them. I don't want them to worry about me more than they do or to feel as if they've failed as parents because I'm having so much trouble. They don't need to know everything, and I can't tell them. In a perfect world, there wouldn't be that barrier of information."

Delia respects her parents' beliefs, while not adhering to them in her own life, but what if you find your parents' backgrounds and perspectives flawed? Kenneth, who is in his late forties, becomes acerbic when he talks about his mother's narrow-mindedness and religious dogma: "She's the product of a blue-blooded, old-line Boston family that believes what is right is very clear and that who is wrong is just about everyone who is not part of the inner core of families with similar breeding. She's judgmental and has immovable ideas about what is proper behavior, what is acceptable and what is not. She balances her snobbery by believing she's a very Christian woman. There are an awful lot of people who have parents like my mother, self-absorbed and threatened by what's going on in the world.

16

They have so many unresolved conflicts and 'stuff' of their own that they've never lived authentic lives, and they can't allow anyone else to live an authentic life. My wife and I are committed to breaking the old-line mold with our children."

Your History Together

Your own childhood history and the parent-child interaction temper your current relationship with your parents. Your attitudes toward your parents may be based on how they behaved when you were a child rather than on their present personalities. Many parents become less authoritative and more relaxed as they and their children age.

When Michael was growing up, he was intimidated by his father's stern and unbending attitudes. Like many parents, his dad worried about what Michael would become and how he would provide for a family. Often it felt to Michael as if it was his father's way or no way, so he avoided his father whenever he had a problem or a decision to make. His father has been much less dogmatic since his son married, but Michael still keeps his distance, only talking to his father about sports or insignificant things about his day. But with his mother, he says, "I talk about family; she asks about my in-laws, we talk about her friends or mine. I feel closer to my mom. I can relate to her on a human, personal level. My mother was the person you could run to for cover, and that stuck with me."

Even when a parent modifies the way he or she treats you, there may be some backsliding. Sally, a thirty-six-year-old foreign language professor, faces a parent who always took pride in being the head of the household. But he still tries to give orders to and make decisions for his adult children as if they were eight years old. When Sally's opinion differs from her father's and he begins to take charge, she explains her position. He relents, but the next time there's a disagreement, he reverts to the same old I'm-running-the-show tactics. Sally says, "His need to control is not malicious; it's a habit. It's more what he thinks is right, what he grew up with. We're moving in the direction of an equal playing field, but only because I'm working on it."

WHY COMMIT TO IMPROVING YOUR RELATIONSHIP?

- To liberate yourself from your "child" role.
- To learn about and understand your parents as people.
- To reduce your levels of guilt.
- To eliminate conflict and tensions.
- To establish stability and emotional security.
- To simply have more fun being together.

Making Choices, Initiating Change

Once you've acknowledged your parents' history, identified their personal demons and dilemmas, and have some understanding of the way you interact with them, you've set the stage to make major and minor changes. You have the power to choose how you want to relate to your parents and how much contact you have with them.

When Helen was a child, she thought her mother was

perfect. But when Helen became a teenager, her views switched. "I didn't want to be close anymore," recalls the twenty-nine-year-old aspiring actress. "When I was a teenager, my mother and I didn't speak for days on end. She drove my sister and me everywhere, and I was embarrassed in front of my friends. I told my mother not to speak when my friends were in the car. We resorted to writing letters to each other; notes were our only form of communication my entire junior year of high school. By then my mother had divorced my alcoholic father and had been a single parent for several years. At the time I only saw comfort in other families, intact families without the problems of alcoholism and divorce. After I grew up and realized how much she did for me and why she had rules, we became a team; we consult each other. She didn't change, I did."

Pamela had been estranged from her father, who abandoned her and her sisters for five years during their early childhood. As an adult, she made a conscious decision to be available for her father. She believes he needs to know someone cares about him. "I don't think he has any friends and he doesn't take care of himself because there are no women in his life. My sisters have little tolerance for him. They visit him only when they have a financial emergency, knowing he will come to their rescue. I talk to him once a week." Pamela makes the effort to close the gap created during the years her father was absent.

There are also times when you may make choices about the extent of your involvement with parents based on the need to protect yourself, your partner, or your children. Ryan lives hundreds of miles from his family because the distance makes it easier to keep his homosexuality from them. "I love my parents and siblings and enjoy being with them for a week or two at a time. I cannot risk them rejecting me if I tell them I'm gay. Being secretive is a source of great frustration; I have to be careful how I act around them, but I feel I've made the right decision for me."

Invasions into your life frequently require standing firm and going against a controlling parent. When David, thirty-three, was planning his honeymoon, his father tried to dictate the destination. As in most things, David's father attempted to manipulate his son by offering to pay for the honeymoon, but only if David and Kay, who had their hearts set on Italy, honeymooned in Israel. David's father drove a hard bargain, and as tempting as the offer was, David thanked his father for the generous offer but firmly told him he and Kay would pay for the honeymoon themselves. After so many years of doing everything his father's way, David liked the feeling of doing something his way, of not being railroaded.

Although parents often mellow in relation to their children, if yours haven't, you can establish new patterns that will change the way you interact. Of course change takes time; however, as Julia found out, when you express yourself, you create a safe environment for others to do the same. "My mother was never given the tools to communicate. I was always looking for affection from her. If I had a husband and five children, I'd still want that affection, because I'll always be her daughter," admits Julia.

Julia told her mother how she felt, but realized that if she wanted her mother to say, "I love you," she had to say it first. "If I wanted a hug or physical affection from her, I had to tackle her—I'm taller and bigger. It's been years since that conversation and now she says 'I love you' on the phone first. I value every single time she does it. I'm glad I didn't hold a grudge or hold back; I opened up, and then she opened up. I think we've connected more in that way."

In the same vein, you may need to revise your expectations because you can't totally remake someone's personality. Akiko, a thirty-year-old costume designer, grew up envying her cousins' extremely close relationship with their mother. Akiko's aunt is very open, and she expresses herself easily. Akiko longed to be able to talk to her mother, but realized that kind of turnaround was unlikely. Akiko changed her goal, deciding to become more understanding and accepting of the way her mother is. When Akiko's father died last year, her mother was very disconnected from her feelings. Akiko looks at her more pragmatically these days, saying to herself, That's how she handles change. "I encourage her to do things that make her happy rather than expecting her to be this warm, completely different person," she says. "My new approach has made her more comfortable, and that helps her open up a bit more than she used to."

At this point you may be thinking, "My dad's impossible. He'll never see my position." Or, "You don't know my mother! There's no changing her." However, it is possible to improve the most difficult or estranged relationships— if you decide to. You can pick up a relationship midstream and work with what you have. Alexia, thirty, had not been on speaking terms with her mother for most of the fifteen years since her mother and father divorced. Before her own marriage Alexia was able to let go of her bitterness and accept the choices her mother made to leave her children with their father. Alexia and her mother have developed a new relationship that has been taking shape slowly over the past two years. "My mother bridged the gap by flying in to come to my wedding, a step forward she had been unable or unwilling to take previously and that meant a lot to me. My relationship with my mother is a long-term project, an important one as I start my own family."

As you determine the path your relationship with your parents will take, remember as an adult, you hold significant decision-making power.

EMPOWERING CHOICES

You decide whether or not to
- Stick with the status quo.
- React to or engage with parents.
- Redefine the relationship.
- Think positively or negatively about it.
- Change how you interact with your parents.

Still Your Parents

Although achieving a more peerlike relationship with parents demands attitude adjustments and new ground rules, some things don't change. There's little question that parents remain your biggest fans and harshest critics—that they continue to praise and to criticize. Undoubtedly, you continue to want your parents' approval—no matter what your age or level of independence or success. In short, your parents' opinions remain extremely important.

Stephanie, thirty-five, the cofounder of a successful dot-com, wonders if she seeks her parents' recognition "because I was such a bad kid that I have to prove what a good kid I am now. I never hurt any person, property, or anything of that nature, but I definitely had a very strong will, a mind of my own. I grew up quickly, and now I sometimes regress into full-blown childhood," she says with a chuckle. "When I was quoted in the newspaper recently, I didn't call my business partner to say, 'Hey, we got a great piece in the *L.A. Times*,' I called my parents and said, 'I'm in the *L.A. Times*! Aren't you proud? Aren't you proud?' I need that affirmation for some reason."

Sometimes, more than approval, you need a parent's backing or confirmation for what you plan to do. Julia decided at a late date to break her engagement. The wedding invitations had been ordered, caterers booked, flowers selected, the dress ready for its second fitting. Julia says, "I couldn't make the final decision until I talked to my parents, and I talked to them before I told my fiancé. I didn't need their approval, but I needed their understanding. I still haven't been able to ask them how much money they lost."

In times of crisis, you may want to turn to parents—one if not both of them—for guidance and support. Corrie, a law firm librarian and thirty-three-year-old recovering drug addict, relied on her parents, particularly her father, to help her overcome her drug problem. "Here's a man who never tried pot, and one day I tell him that I'm a heroin addict," Corrie begins. "He didn't freak out, he took it in stride; he asked me what *we* do about it. I saw him cry for the first time in his life. To be in your sixties and be able to talk about your emotions to help your child is pretty amazing. He supported me through the really rough recovery periods, and our relationship grew stronger. He's an incredibly kind person and the person I look up to most in the world. Whatever happens, he goes with it. I like being with my mother, but it's easy between my father and me. He's become the person I go to, he's my best friend," she enthuses.

You are linked to your parents forever, but can your relationship with them be perfect? Probably not, but you can improve it dramatically and optimize its potential. However, having the most respectful and congenial relationships with parents doesn't mean that you won't have painful memories or that you won't ever disagree with each other again.

The very nature of the parent-child bond cultivates irritants that you want to diffuse or clear away entirely as your relationship progresses to a better place. Should distressing feelings or situations recur, you can delicately set new parameters. Parents can stress you only as much as you let them. You have the same level of control over a parent as you do a friend, a difficult concept to grasp and put into action primarily because you expect more, you want more, you wish for more from a parent.

BEFORE INITIATING ANY CHANGE

- Compare your parents' backgrounds and life experiences with yours.
- Determine how and why their thinking may be different from yours.
- Understand that change takes time.
- Overlook your parents' flaws, if that will help move the relationship in a positive direction.
- Keep in mind that your function is to help the relationship operate smoothly.
- Consider your relationship as ever changing.

TWO

Still Driving You Crazy

Without thinking too hard or too long, you can probably make a list of unnerving things your parents do and say that cause friction and discord. Does your mother still remind you to comb your hair? Do your parents persist in passing unacceptable judgment on the people you date—or don't date—or on the person you have chosen to live with or marry? On the other hand, your parents may fawn and fuss over your partner to such an extent that you sometimes feel they actually prefer that person to you. You may have parents who insist you're in the wrong profession, ignoring completely that you are happy and successful.

Parents can rattle you about your work ethic, lifestyle choices, or your interaction with a sibling, stepparent, or step- and half-siblings. They can shake your confidence in your new hairstyle, the body you spent months sweating into shape, or how you show off that hard-earned figure. There's no end to ways parents can throw you off balance and resurrect old doubts—after all these years. They may continue to lecture, teach, probe, whine, insist, beg, or chastise, no matter how self-sufficient and established you are. If you explain how this makes you feel or ask them to modify their language or behavior, they may say they can't help themselves, or perhaps that they were only kidding or didn't mean it. Parents are good at pressing the buttons that go to the heart of your insecurities.

Parenting behaviors you find offensive are more often than not leftovers from childhood. The tendency to think of you as a baby and to worry about you comes from years of protecting you and feeling concern for your well-being. These are ingrained habits, usually unrecognized by parents themselves, and therefore difficult for them to stop. How successful are your parents at upsetting your equilibrium?

MEASURING YOUR ANNOYANCE THRESHOLD

- Do you bristle inwardly with each parental judgment?
- Do you avoid certain subjects because you fear—or know—what your parent will say?
- Do you lash out at your parent when he or she tries to direct or correct you?
- Do you "tune out" your parent when you hear a criticism start?
- Do you tense before a visit with your parent?
- Do you spend an inordinate amount of time dressing or putting on makeup before seeing your parents?
- Do you feel compelled to put your house or apartment in tip-top shape before they visit?

If you answered yes to any question, one or both of your parents are "getting to you."

So Annoying

You have options, some of which may be used in combination, for dealing with manipulation, control, intense scrutiny, excessive worry, and overprotectiveness. You can accept how things are, avoid problem areas whenever you can, change your perception of a situation, modify your attitude about a situation, walk away from a situation, or try to modify your parent's behavior.

ALWAYS THE BABY

"I'll get the cab, you sit, you wait," Alice's mother instructed.

"Mother, you sit and I'll get the cab," Alice replied. Her mother dismissed Alice's plea with a wave of her umbrella and raced out to the curb in the pouring rain to hail a taxi.

Alice slumped into a chair in her mother's apartment lobby—a chair similar to the one she had occupied in inclement weather growing up in that same New York City apartment building. Her eighty-six-year-old mother had been fussing over and protecting Alice for nearly six decades and wasn't about to stop.

Rather than insisting, Alice acquiesced; it's sometimes simpler to accept how things are, especially since her mother was spry and healthy enough to hail a cab. Her mother wanted to pamper her, unaware that Alice disliked being treated like a child. On minor issues, as in Alice's case, indulge your parent or approach the situation with a sense of humor, as Harry does. "I'm in my seventies, and my ninety-five-year-old mother tells me what to do," says Harry. "It does seem a bit absurd, but that's the way it is. The sad part," Harry laughs, "is that I have been known to listen to her."

No matter how hard you try to change a parent's approach, your parents may refuse to acknowledge your age, maturity, or independence. They excuse their "transgressions" because they believe and may say, "You'll always be my child, you're still my baby."

Morgan wants to share her life with her mother and ask for her mother's advice as if she were a friend, but she is foiled because her mother has her frozen at a certain age. "She seems not to realize that I'm thirty-seven and interacts with me as if I were twelve," laments Morgan. "I feel she doesn't know who I am because she's stuck. I haven't had much luck in changing our relationship. I've talked to her about it and suggested we go to therapy together, but she's content with our relationship as it is and claims she doesn't have the emotional energy to go through counseling."

Monica is similarly frustrated by her mother's attitude, but Monica is angry, too. "I'm thirty-four, and my mother still says, 'Oh, you're my baby; I carried you for nine months, give me a hug.'" Monica seethes when she talks about being babied. "Morning sickness, labor pains, and nursing give a mother rights for just so long."

It's quite possible that Monica's mother is oblivious to her behavior, just as your parent may be. Telling a parent how you feel or what you don't like is often sufficient to change a parent's action. Lydia is fifty-four years old and the youngest child in the family. Until he died two years ago, her father called her his baby, even in front of her business friends. Whenever he said it, Lydia could feel herself getting irritated. "I wish I had just asked him not to do it," she says. "That would have eliminated a lot of the tension between us, and I think he would have listened."

INCESSANT WORRY

Like parental "babying," incessant worrying can be equally exasperating. Are you getting an annual checkup, exercising enough, eating too much or too little, sleeping eight hours, getting out, working too hard? Your parent may hone in on one worry or embrace them all.

The words *worry* and *parent* seem to be practically synonymous. Worry can be so pervasive that it becomes a personality trait. If your parent is a chronic worrier, try explaining to her that worrying is futile. Judd, who is thirty-two and whose opinions on the environment are sought by government leaders, concludes that he should have told his mother years ago that his brother, sister, and he were going to end up having their own successes and making their own mistakes, no matter how much she worries. Judd's mother has finally gotten to the point where she realizes it doesn't do any good to worry, that her children have done pretty well for themselves.

But Diane, who is forty-nine and a mother herself, believes parents never stop worrying about their offspring. "My middle sister is not married, so my parents worry about her more, but the rest of us have had two marriages, so we keep our parents busy worrying as well. My mother magnifies any situation, but she always did. She's anxious, and that's part of her personality."

Adult children who have fearful, nervous parents may find it beneficial to change their own attitude. Follow the lead of Blake, a thirty-five-year-old television producer at a major network. Blake says of his fretting mother, "She worries about what I eat, but she knows I'm a bit of a fitness fanatic; she worries about my career when she's fully aware that I'm fairly successful. It's nice to have someone worrying about you even when the worry is unfounded."

NOT UP TO SNUFF—INTENSE
PARENTAL SCRUTINY

You may have a parent who measures and evaluates your every decision—or at least it feels that way—a condition that puts a lot of stress on you. When you find yourself spending an inordinate amount of time preparing for a parent's visit, ask yourself how much of the cleanup or attention to your appearance is for you and how much is designed either to thwart parental criticism or to gain parental approval. Women, in particular, often must endure intense examination from their mothers and fathers, but there are ways to reduce the pressure.

Margie, a thirty-eight-year-old designer of teen sportswear, knows her mother's proud of her because she's educated and able to care for herself, but Margie doesn't meet her standards in a lot of regards, particularly housekeeping. When her mother comes to Margie's house, she cleans it. Margie feels she's old enough not to care, but gets annoyed when her mother persists and goes overboard. "On a recent visit she folded my underwear, even though I told her to leave it alone," Margie reports. "On the other hand, when my husband and I moved into a new house and she helped me clean up after the previous owners, who were slobs, I was more than happy to take her help. My new philosophy is, I will enjoy her help—if she is willing to clean my house and it makes her feel good, I will bite my tongue."

The actions and words of a hypercritical parent can be

more difficult to accept, ignore—or excuse. Jessica encounters constant badgering in a range of areas and has for as long as she can remember. Her two children's activities leave her only a few hours a week for herself, but because over the years her mother has made her so concerned about how she looks, she spends them at the gym. "Now she's become focused on my daughter's weight," says Jessica. "She's a kindergartener with a pot-belly, and my mother is second-guessing what I feed her. She made me self-conscious, but I will not allow her to do the same thing to my child."

Rather than agonize, Courtney, thirty-one, took an aggressive approach with her supercritical mother who passes judgment on people's possessions, money, and on the touchy subject of appearances. "It was shocking to her that somebody could be heavy and nice," says Courtney. "When she made comments about my weight, I got very upset and jumped down her throat, so she's labeled me 'overly sensitive.' She believes she has to watch everything she says around me, but if that's what she needs to think, that's fine. She doesn't comment to me anymore because she knows I'll walk away. We've reached a point in our relationship where she talks about other family members instead of attacking me."

Mothers aren't the only ones who focus on body image and fitness. Samantha realized that her father was driven and obsessive, even in retirement. A day doesn't go by when he doesn't work out for an hour, and he's pushy about Samantha following his fitness example. Samantha inherited a tendency to be overweight from her mother and goes through periods of visiting a gym or joining a soccer team with other out-of-shape, thirty-something soccer moms, but her father continues to preach. "He'll say something like, 'Make sure you stay in shape so you don't in-jure yourself!' There's always that one extra thing, how you should be doing something, and then some. He does things as a perfectionist, and he expects some leaning toward per-fection from me."

Samantha has the luxury of coping with her father on the telephone, an option not available to Roxanne, thirty-seven, whose parents live a short car ride away. Roxanne has had to learn new ways to live with her mother's daily inspection, the mind games her mother plays, and her mother's expectations. "If my mother feels my outfit doesn't coordinate by her standards, she says something like, 'Honey, you know that red and yellow don't match. How about the white or beige blouse?' If I say I don't have time to change, she puts on an offended or hurt look to try to guilt me into changing," Roxanne groans. "In the least she wants me to note and appreciate that she's advising me about what's best for me because in her mind I really don't know.

"When I point-blank ask for her opinion, she has none. The game is not to ask, but rather to listen for her cues or outright suggestions and accept them. If I follow her sug-gestions, I'm considered a perfect daughter. Well, I no longer strive to be perfect. It's a lot easier to cope with her perfectionism by understanding that no one is perfect, in-cluding my mother."

Typically, this pattern of expectation is reserved for nuclear family, while parents portray a different persona to others. Outside the family, people turn to Roxanne's mother for objective and compassionate advice. She's one way with her family and another way with everyone else. Roxanne finds her mother's different faces almost as dis-turbing as her criticism and demands.

FOR YOUR OWN GOOD:
MANIPULATION AND CONTROL

Many parents believe they know what is best and right for their offspring and that this justifies their attempts to maneuver and control their adult children. Some parental manipulation may, in fact, be for your own good, but you surely don't want to be on the receiving end. Attempts to mastermind your life may stir feelings of guilt or put you on the defensive. Sometimes the best reaction is to simply acknowledge that you hear what your parent is suggesting.

Your parents may even try to run aspects of your life that have no direct affect on them. When Julia moved out of an apartment she had shared with her boyfriend, she found a smaller place. She was devastated by the breakup, but her mother carried on about the size of the new apartment and ignored Julia's heartbreak. Her mother reminded her repeatedly that her furniture would never fit. "I could have told my mother that at the moment my things weren't important, that I wasn't thinking about the practicalities, but instead I told her I heard what she was saying, and promptly signed the lease. My furniture fit."

Less transparent forms of control are more difficult to handle. Your parent may be a giving, caring person with a manipulative, controlling underbelly, a sharp streak that's well camouflaged. Generally, such a parent is less candid about demands, and you may be more easily tricked into or swayed to follow your parent's demands and feel extreme guilt when you don't.

Lucy's mother is the master of guilt trips, but Lucy sees through her. "If I'm planning a weekend with my husband and in-laws, my mother will dream up a reason to need me that weekend. When I say, 'I'll be with Carter and his parents,' she comes back with, 'Well, you all have a good time. That's what's really important to me—that you're happy and your family is happy.' I know she wants me with her, and I feel horribly guilty."

Pitting one sibling against another is a different tactic some parents use to control their adult children. Morgan's mother, for example, aligns herself first with Morgan, a few weeks later with her brother. She bonds with one child and talks about the other, creating havoc between this brother and sister. When Morgan and her brother called her on it, their mother seemed unaware of how destructive her behavior was or why she did it. Having been told, she figured out that she needed to stop if she wanted to improve her relationship with her grown children.

It may have taken you a while to catch on to your parent's determination to be in charge of your life. Some adult children find that only through therapy do they come to accept a parent's ways, particularly if parental control has been in effect for many years. When a parent's control of your life feels out of hand, it becomes necessary to try to break the pattern, if only to reduce the level of guilt the control creates. With therapy, Heidi recognized her mother's limitations and better understands the forces behind her behavior. When they were fighting, Heidi's mother would punish her by having no contact at all. Arguments were often over something forty-four-year-old Heidi was doing that her mother didn't think sent out good images of her children, meaning a good image of herself. Heidi's mother is much more concerned with how things affect her than how they affect other people, including her children. Therapy helped Heidi see how her mother's uptight society family caused her to worry about how her children presented themselves to the world.

"I don't doubt that she loves me," says Heidi, "but now

I am able to be amused by her attempts to control my every move, to be amused when she thinks we're not dressed properly for a function or my children are ill-behaved. I've accepted that she's stubborn and strong, so I no longer feel compelled to make her otherwise. The most useful thing in messy situations with my mother, when she's obstinate or has to have things her way, is being able to keep my sense of humor, to laugh about whatever it is, and to stay away from her until she calms down."

Ruthless attempts to control you are better answered by putting temporary distance between you and a parent than by walking away permanently. Because of the intense bond between a parent and child, rejecting a parent is, for most adult children, nearly impossible. Kenneth, forty-eight and a banker, tries, but knows he will ultimately fail in spite of the fact that he's emotionally at his wit's end with his mother and can find little to like about her. "They should have named the narcissist hall of fame after her," he says. "I actually think she has a personality disorder, but it's never been diagnosed. What she can't control freaks her out. I've reached the point that she is no longer welcome in my home, and I say, 'I'm finished,' but I don't know how long I'll stand firm on my vow."

If you have a parent similar to Heidi's or Kenneth's mother, you can distance yourself by seeing him or her less often and by reducing the number of times you talk on the telephone. In this way, there is less opportunity for conflicts that bring out different forms of parental control. You can also achieve a level of emotional distance once you recognize your own needs and separate them from your parent's needs. When you honor and enforce your own needs, a parent will be less able to dictate your course. You want nontoxic interaction with your parents, but when loss of control over your own life, insults, or hurt feelings are what you come away with, it's time to move the relationship in another direction.

CHECKLIST FOR MANAGING ANNOYING BEHAVIOR

- Evaluate your parent's awareness of his or her behavior:
  - Is she well meaning?
  - Is he trying to be helpful?
  - Is she overreacting?
  - Get another opinion if you feel you need it.
  - Consider if you are being too sensitive.
- Tell a parent when he or she is being too critical, controlling, or demanding:
  - Point out behaviors you don't like.
  - Put into words how her comments and actions make you feel.
  - Ask your parent to change or stop a behavior that upsets you.
  - Look for humor in the situation.
- Rely on your own judgment to assure yourself that your actions and decisions are sensible.

Addressing Trouble Spots

The list of parents' personality traits you may have to work around can be daunting. A parent who is a chronic worrier, judgmental or critical, removed, selfish, insensitive or too sensitive, argumentative, or who has several of these traits is likely to have difficulties with adult offspring. You have the option to make a concrete change or to alter the way you think about your parent under given circumstances. Either approach will help reduce the friction and make it easier to jump the emotional hurdles.

TAKING ACTION

Removing or modifying just one seemingly small irritant opens the door to more comfortable interactions with your parents. Sophia and her mother do some things very differently. Often they argued in stores, and Sophia felt disturbed and embarrassed. Instead of subjecting herself to repeated shopping expeditions, Sophia, who is forty-three years old, narrowed the focus of what she does with her mother to areas in which they have no conflict. "My mother and I have different rhythms; we play at different speeds. She has to touch everything and ask salespeople a million questions, whether or not she's planning to buy. Shopping with her was torture for me. She's fun to have dinner with, to babble with about politics, but I'll never shop with her again." Sophia walked away from a situation that caused her considerable stress and strained her relationship with her mother.

Morgan has no patience for her mother's stream of inane phone calls that interrupt her at the office and almost always have to do with her aches and pains or what's on sale at the grocery story. As soon as Morgan hears her mother's voice, she becomes defensive, irritable, and short. Although Morgan can't change her mother, she can change her mother's behavior so it is less invasive and upsetting. Among her options: Morgan could ask her mother not to call her at work, explaining that she is irritable on the phone because she is too busy to talk; she might ask her mother to call her at home at a specific time when it's likely she'll be less pressed and more relaxed. Morgan could also ask her mother to e-mail her. E-mail forces the writer to see what she is saying; in an E-mail her mother might limit her chitchat. On Morgan's end, with E-mail in front of her she will have time to process what she reads, minimizing the chance she will overreact. Any of these approaches will remove the irritant from the middle of Morgan's day and ease this particular glitch in her relationship with her mother.

Jessica characterizes her mother as insensitive and the things she says as venomous. "On my birthday, a few months after I had had a tumor removed, she said, 'I hope you realize how lucky you are.' The gynecologist had assured me that it was safe to have another child, but my mother said, 'You should not have another baby. It will be a burden, and you can't afford it.' This is the way she thinks; she doesn't consider how what she says wounds me. When I ask her why she says the things she does, her response is, 'Well, I see this conversation is getting us nowhere.'"

Her sister, Julia, doesn't get upset about their mother's heartless comments; she takes her behavior more in stride. She laughs about it. Julia doesn't feel the need to protect herself from her mother, but for Jessica to cope with her mother, she must keep their conversations on a superficial level.

Highly sensitive parents are as problematic as insensitive ones. You must tiptoe around their feelings, weigh their moods, and choose your words and actions carefully. This is the parent who is likely to interpret almost anything you say negatively. For example, suggest your parent move to a warm climate for his retirement years, and you may be met with, "You don't want me near you." With a sensitive parent, literally anything can add another layer to the wall between you.

Rebecca's mother is easily offended and uses the cold-shoulder approach whenever she is. According to Rebecca, her mother's stories are very boring and go on forever. If Rebecca tries to rush her mother or asks her to get to the point quickly, her mother's feelings get hurt, and she won't speak to Rebecca for days. The longest time they didn't talk was two weeks, but whenever they pick up the phone, they pretend nothing ever happened. Rebecca can change this pattern by altering her own approach. Rather than acting as if they hadn't had a conflict, she might ask her mother what offended her during their last conversation or concede that she hurt her mother's feelings, but explain why it happened.

ACTIONS TO TAKE WITH AN OVERLY SENSITIVE PARENT

- Find out what you did by saying, "I need to know so I can understand, so I can prevent it from happening again."
- Tell your parent that not speaking is unacceptable.
- Explain how you feel: "When you do or say this, I feel this way."
- Ask, "What can I do to change or improve our relationship?"

If you and your parents have a history of disagreeing or are personality mismatches, the pattern is likely to continue until you do something to stop it. Lillian's father does not approve of her life choices; he is religious, and she is not. He wishes she were married and had children. As a result, their relationship was argumentative, but Lillian found the constant discord too upsetting. "I believe he thinks getting a rise out of me shows me he loves me. I don't agree. I recently decided to stop arguing it. It takes two to argue." Lillian smiles conspiratorially.

In most instances, the only way your parent will change is if you point out what is wrong. In the past, Amy and her dad were always up for an argument; they related by picking on each other. After Amy married and moved away, she didn't want to be his sparring buddy during the brief time she spent with him. When he tries to get her goat now, she tells him to stop. Amy can be very honest with her father because there's part of him that really does appreciate her straightforwardness.

Amy, who had many conflicts with her father when she was younger, decided to turn the relationship around. She believes "someone can change if he tries. My father has changed, but mostly because I have. Once in a while we'll fall back into our old patterns, but for the most part being together has been a lot smoother, a lot more fun since I told him arguing upsets me."

ALTERING YOUR THINKING

Parents have their own natures, and at times changing or compensating for your parent's failing feels hopeless. But revisiting, rethinking, and readjusting your approach may be all that is needed. Granted, with some parents no amount of cajoling or persuading will change that parent's approach, making it all the more essential for you to change yours. Once you understand the reasons behind your parent's actions, it's usually easier to reconcile how things should be in your own mind. And there is always the chance that your new approach may influence your parent in such a way that enduring patterns or conflicts disappear.

Thea and her mother have spent most of Thea's life in battle over just about everything. "I used to fight with my mom, but often the emotional cost of defying her was too high," Thea says. "For a long time, I tried putting my foot down, but she gets hysterical, and there's no changing her mind. A few years ago I decided that in Mom's world there is no logic. Now, since I don't see her that much, we can hang out and be the best of friends for three or four days doing whatever she wants. We take micro-vacations somewhere close, since we are both very busy. We may get into a discussion about where to eat, and I'd rather not go to her choice, but since I started saying to myself, 'I don't need to engage in this issue,' we've gotten along better. I don't have to make her admit when I'm right. It's just not that important."

If you want to maximize parents' robust years, it may be time to adopt a new attitude, as Thea has done, or to forgive your parents, as Janice, a forty-nine-year-old interior designer, did. When Janice was eight months pregnant, her mother tried to extract a promise from her that she would not allow her father (from whom her mother had been divorced for two decades) to come to the hospital when Janice's son was born. Janice was so upset, she worried she might be damaging the baby. Janice recalls her mother's demand seventeen years later: "My mother badgered me to comply with her wishes, but the sting has disappeared. I don't feel it anymore. She was in a crazed state; she likes being in the victim role. I don't like that part of her, but that's not the most important part of who

Tools for Addressing Trouble Spots

- Avoid topics and conversations you know are problematic.
- Decide what's worth arguing about and what you should ignore.
- Acknowledge what your parent says, but don't overreact.
- Weigh how much of the annoyance comes from your parent and how much is actually pressure you are putting on yourself.
- Bear in mind, it's not important that you always be "right."
- Don't be afraid to ruffle a parent's feathers.
- Be aware of what you want from your parent and what he or she is capable of or prepared to give.

she is—she's generous, loving, warm, good company, and she loves being with me—so I overlook her faults and focus on positive things about her. If I didn't, she'd drive me nuts."

When you reframe your thinking about old grudges, irritating parent behaviors, and attitudes, what you see as painful personality defects and horrible disappointment lose their edge. Even a relationship with huge emotional problems can be reexamined in a positive light. Few achieve the twist in thinking more successfully than Cynthia, a fifty-year-old gynecologist whose mother's parenting bordered on abusive. Cynthia's mother is an uneducated, bitter woman who took her frustrations out on her children and resented Cynthia's ambitions to rise above poverty. The more Cynthia succeeded in school or demonstrated a talent, the more chores her mother gave her. The harder her mother made her life, the more Cynthia wanted to achieve her goals, and the more strength she found to pursue them, and all the while their relationship became more violent.

"I could certainly be angry," Cynthia says of the past, "but I turned my mother's failings into motivation for my success. As a grown-up, I've determined that she, in a perverted way, made me a success. Her negativism was so widespread, I reversed her mindset in my own head and made it work to my benefit."

Coping with Relationship Gaps

Relationship gaps form when your parents are not giving you what you need in the way of emotional support, understanding, or affection or in the way of practical support, such as assistance when you could use it. As you become increasingly independent, the gaps become more apparent. (Having children of your own can be the impetus for reevaluating your upbringing and trying to figure how your relationship with your parent stalled or arrived at its current, disturbing place.) Relationship vacuums can be corrected, or at the least modified, with the same tools you use to deal with your parents' irksome behaviors.

A planned effort may be needed to reach an emotionally distant parent. Sophia's family didn't do a lot of hugging or touching, and Sophia can't remember a time her mother hugged her until her mother started imitating Sophia being affectionate with her friends and nieces. "My mother is learning from her children and grandchildren. I don't blame my mother because her pain is locked in multiple tiers, stemming back to parents who didn't show affection and horrific family suicides."

Knowing her mother's history explained much of the reason for her lack of affection. Sophia's mother supplied enough information so her daughter could accept the void and try to do something about it. But at times you have no idea what causes your parents to be withholding or unresponsive. In that case, it takes guts for you to ask hard questions that will clear the air and allow you to understand and perhaps forgive your parent.

Olivia, thirty-three, believes her mother never wanted to be a parent. "She was so unhappy being at home with two kids. She must have asked herself every day what she was doing in a house with children. She would go 'psycho' for no reason and start screaming and hitting us. My dad never stepped in to protect or stand up for us. She got out as soon as she possibly could, right before we hit puberty, and my sister and I lived with my dad.

"She wanted us to be involved in her life, but once she declared she was a lesbian, visiting her every other week was a mortifying experience. I talked to her as little as possible until I had my daughter, and then I was able to tell her how upset I was with her. I managed to tell her the obvious, that we've never gotten along, and I didn't know how to relate to her. I couldn't ask her what I really wanted to know: why she had children when she really didn't want them. She never even tried to hide that fact. I thought about asking my dad, but he's very cynical and shut down about my mother."

Answers to questions are frequently contrary to what you thought or believed. Sometimes it's a relief for your parent to give answers, and answers can remove the unknown that is blocking your relationship. If Olivia could ask these questions, she might discover that her mother didn't realize she was a lesbian until after she had her children. She might discover that more than anything, her mother wants a relationship with Olivia but doesn't know where to begin. Olivia's questions might be just the jolt their relationship needs.

Not asking leaves the relationship barren, relegated to where it was, with neither parent nor adult child getting what they want. As Lindsay states, "It's not going to do any good to go back; we have to move forward. I need the courage to tell my mom I love her. That's something we didn't do in our family. I would hate myself if something happened to her, and I never said those words."

Parents who remain unaware of or insensitive to their children's feelings intensify the gap in the relationship. Rebecca is thirty-three years old, the mother of two toddlers and an infant, and perplexed by her mother's lack of empathy. Rebecca had had a particularly difficult parenting day, the kind of day during which the children whine, spill milk, and don't follow any instruction or order. The baby was teething, and by evening Rebecca was exhausted and depressed. If it weren't for her children's peaceful faces when they finally did go to sleep, Rebecca was sure she would have walked out of the house or done something drastic to herself. The next day Rebecca's mother called on her cell phone from Nordstrom. Rebecca explained how unhappy she was and what the day before had been like, but her mother interrupted to ask if the children needed any clothes. Her mother hadn't heard a word Rebecca said, or if she had, she didn't know how to respond. Rebecca wanted her mother to be aware of the state she was in and to care enough to call back to see if she were feeling any better. "It's been forty-eight hours and she hasn't called," reports Rebecca. "I don't know why I'm annoyed; she never talked about emotions with her own mother and certainly not with me. My husband's mom would have called twice by now if she knew I was feeling overwhelmed." Parents like Rebecca's may not realize you want their emotional support. Rather than being upset with their lack of empathy, be straightforward. Let a parent know that her behavior upsets you. In the future, it's far more likely she will pay attention to your need.

Having a parent's support or involvement in your adult life is not something to take for granted. There's a whole culture of parents that thinks parents should mind their own business and feels strongly about staying out of their adult children's lives, especially their social lives. From their perspective, their motives are admirable: They don't want to make waves, so they don't ask a lot of questions or interfere in any noticeable or aggressive way. But you may want your careful parents more involved, so you feel less detached from them. Parents who tread ever so cautiously can't know who you've become and what you need from them unless you tell them. They aren't mind readers. You may have to give your parents permission to probe so they can share your life.

Julia would like her parents to ask questions. "I'm afraid they think they can't. I feel I could reveal information, but they don't ask me deep emotional questions. Every now and then, my dad will have a Hallmark moment; he'll ask if I'm happy. I'd like them to be less afraid to dig a little deeper. I'd love it if they got nosy with my life, but I guess I have to tell them." She does.

Ways to Bridge Relationship Gaps

- Tell your parents you would like them more involved in your life, and in what specific areas.
- Give parents permission to ask questions.
- Understand your parent's limitations.
- Change your expectations of your parents.
- Attend counseling together.
- Focus on the aspects of your relationship that work well.
- Clear the air by discussing old or new issues that bother you.
- Ask others to help you keep perspective.
- Use partners and close relatives to fulfill needs your parents can't.

PROTECTING THE GAP, FILLING THE VOIDS

In some adult child-parent relationships, the gap provides the adult child with a safety zone that reduces the chances of conflict and discomfort for either party. Filtering or withholding information can be an effective tool for keeping the relationship sound. With particularly intrusive parents, such an approach makes good sense because it downplays conflict and promotes harmony.

Kathrine, thirty-one and single, has learned to reveal only what she wants her parents to know. If she's dating someone new and is not sure where the relationship is going, she doesn't tell them much about him, except to say, "'There's this guy I'm dating.' Any drop of detail sets off an interrogation."

About the facts of her dating life, Devin says, "I know what my mother's answers and comments will be. She's very traditional, and I know she will give me advice I shouldn't listen to. I have been in relationships that I know are not good for me, and she advises me, 'Just stick with him and tell him he's right. You don't want to be alone the rest of your life.' I steer clear of dating conversations and talk to her about other things."

As protection, you may decide to make discussion of your career, your spouse, in-laws, or major purchases off-limits to your parents. Some even relocate as safeguard from parents who insinuate themselves too aggressively into their lives. You may have to get used to the idea that it is best if your parents aren't involved in every facet of your life and find other ways to fill the voids.

When the people who raised you do not or are unable to meet your needs, relying on others is an acceptable, smart way to compensate. Spouses, partners, in-laws, and friends fill not only emotional voids but also voids connected to physical and practical support—from mentoring you in business to helping care for your newborn or frisky toddlers. Having someone stand in for your parent reduces the number of needs you would otherwise look to your parent to fulfill, and lessens the pressure on the relationship. This can strengthen your adult child-parent connection and prevent it from disintegrating further. Talking to someone other than a parent may or may not resolve the particular problem you have with your parent, but people usually feel better when they are heard.

Megan's parents are very traditional in a 1950s sense; they don't like to delve into or express their feelings. Although they were loving toward their five children, Megan, thirty-five and the youngest, doesn't think either of them was equipped emotionally to have so many off-spring. The lack of emotional ties between parents and children and between the siblings helps Megan accept her parents' reaction to her child. "When my daughter was born, and beforehand, my parents knew the baby had physical problems. I felt very alone because they didn't know how to help me deal with the baby's illness. They couldn't even mention it. But my husband listened to me and helped me adjust to what we were facing."

Spouse support extends to helping you spot patterns and pitfalls. Lucy's husband alerts her to the guilt trips her parents lay on her. "When my parents attempt to manipulate me, he asks me to be sure I want to do whatever they are asking and am not doing it just to please them. His observations help stop me from jumping at every demand my parents make."

A partner's support can go beyond advice and comfort; it can be the salve that soothes you when your relationship with a parent is insincere or distant. Courtney has a mother who mouths the words of support, but doesn't deliver. "My mother says things like, 'Anything you go through, I'm here for you,' but she isn't. I get support and compliments from my husband, and that helps my relationship with her."

In-laws fill in relationship holes, too, as providers of affection and support, mentors and role models. When daughters-in-law and mothers-in-law and fathers-in-law and sons-in-law become close, the friendships yield high dividends. Kim says of her husband and father, "They beat each other up verbally with one witty comment after the other. I love listening. I know it makes my father so happy, since his relationship with my brothers isn't great, and it makes my husband happy, because his father was so humorless and serious and strict."

Kenneth found surprising support from his father-in-law. "My father-in-law is the type of man you would expect to be incredibly blunt, and he is about some things, yet he turned out to be sensitive, aware, and helpful. In terms of my adult mentoring, I've had far more mentoring from my father-in-law than from my father."

Courtney, whose value system is the antithesis of her mother's, relies on her mother-in-law for direction. Once Courtney realized she didn't have to be like her mother, she spent less time with her and more with her mother-in-law, whom Courtney describes as completely selfless and genuine. Her mother-in-law doesn't judge people by their money and is more able to compromise than her mother. "My mother-in-law has a job, and to my mother a woman having to work is the worst fate," Courtney notes. "In those areas, my mother-in-law is definitely my role model."

Some gaps can't be filled, and some disappointments are too egregious to accept. Thea's parents divorced when she was only seven, and her history with her father was a constant trial. He complained so much when he had to take her sister and her places that Thea made up her mind at a very young age that she wasn't going to ask him for anything when she visited.

Thea's mother waived her alimony in exchange for college tuition for their children, but Thea says, "I would go to register, and the school would not have his check. I went through that every semester; and he refused to send food money. I had to see my father twice a year to beg for money while we had lunch at his private club with annual dues of over $10,000.

"I had always planned to change my name when I got married, because I didn't feel a link to his name, but I did it when I finished medical school instead. Apparently this is not so rare; another friend did it, and we had a big party. I've had a great education; I have lots of friends and one great parent, my mom. I've changed my name and moved on. At a certain point anger gets boring," she says. "I'm going to put my dad behind me and move forward and have a great life. You can't do much with a parent who rejects you."

Your New, Leading Role

You are the final judge of what bothers you in relationships with your parents; your feelings and opinion are the only ones that mean anything, regardless of their accuracy. Adopt an approach similar to Jessica's: "I have to face the facts and do what I can to salvage (or improve) the relationship." If you can recognize or accept personality flaws in your parents, you'll be better equipped to reprogram irritating weak spots and make the relationship one you can live with.

As the disturbing, vexing, provoking, or simply annoying elements of your relationship become more manageable or acceptable, you may find that your parents actually begin to change. Parents may mellow, redefine their priorities, and the relationship parameters get new definitions. Will a parent's irritating actions and comments simply vanish? Unlikely. Will every gap in the relationship be filled? Probably not. But as Amy put it: "The things that annoy me about my father are the things I grew up with and didn't like, and still don't particularly care for. Does it get in the way of our relationship? No. Because that's who he is. When you love someone, you love good and bad." Eliminating or moderating the things about your parents that still drive you crazy prepares you—and them—for greatly improved communication and more satisfying time spent together.

GUIDELINES FOR ESTABLISHING YOUR NEW ROLE

- Believe you have the power to determine your new role.
- Decide what you can and cannot accept in and from your parents.
- Let your parents know how their behaviors affect you.
- Explore your parents' willingness to modify their behaviors.
- Inform parents how you plan to change interactions with them.
- Be willing to try out roles until you find one that works for you.

THREE

Staying Connected

Most adult children and their parents are eager to have ongoing, gratifying relationships, but you no doubt have many pressing priorities beyond finding time to talk to and visit with your parents. You are splintered in assorted directions: focused on friends, personal pursuits, growing families, and/or bustling careers. Finding the time to spend with your parents often means juggling your commitments and schedules and dealing with other people's feelings, needs, and desires. Although you may have a hard time recognizing it, the ball—and momentum of the relationship—is almost always in your court. You determine how much time you devote to them and, to a large degree, how that time is spent. If you have a busy life, it is far more likely that your parents are waiting for an invitation from you.

Phillip, a single thirty-two-year-old New York City lawyer working his way up the legal ladder, lives in the adult child perpetual time bind with its good intentions and requisite guilt. He admits that his career ambitions often lead to neglect of his parents. "My mother recently completed her doctorate in the learning disabilities field and wants to start an awareness program for parents. I have the contacts to help her, and we're going to work together to set up a program. The hitch is when.

"I work too many hours a week and too many weekends, so I hardly ever visit. Calling is the best I can do these days, and that isn't often enough. I want to help her with this project because I see how important it is to her, and the best part is, I'm in a position to be of real help. I can do more than offer encouraging platitudes. I just have to find the time."

Phillip's mother, Victoria, fifty-five, recognizes her son's time restraints, but his lack of support for her project hurts nonetheless. She's thrilled when her son calls, and she knows he wants to help. "He says he'll come over to discuss it, but he doesn't have time for me right now. I have a life, too, but it would be nice to speak to him on some regular basis. And seeing him . . . who knows when?"

Demanding careers, spouses, partners, children, social lives, volunteer efforts, exercise, dental and medical appointments, car repairs, and house or apartment chores vie for immediate attention. On any given day, your list might include several of these responsibilities, any one of which can take an inordinate amount of your time and emotional energy, leaving little left over for a parent.

It may help you to make time for your parents if you consider their perspective. Unless you've sent a child to college, witnessed your offspring's wedding, or watched him move to another state or part of the country, it's difficult to grasp the complex upheaval most parents experience in giving up the parenting role that defined them for so many years. In the years that came before, being close and knowing what was going on in your child's life was simply part of a normal day.

Stephanie's parents quietly but firmly held onto the parenting role, not wanting to distance themselves from their children. Logic and money issues weighed strongly in favor of them selling the home Stephanie and her brother grew up in and moving somewhere with a lower cost of living, so they could keep more of the money from the sale of the house. But her parents refused to do it because they didn't want to be away from their children. "I argued that I didn't see them that much anyway," said Stephanie, "and reminded them how they complain that I never spend the night, but if they lived out of state, I would have no choice. My brother and I thought our mother was insisting they stay here, but when I pressed my dad to move, he said, 'I don't want to be away from you and your brother either.'"

Your parents want to be acknowledged and appreciated, and one way to satisfy this almost universal desire is the simple act of staying in touch on a regular basis. Even parents who appear completely independent of their grown children want to be included in their offsprings' lives. In spite of what parents may say, their children usually still come first in what may seem to be parents' full lives. Having your parents actively involved in your life may actually turn out to be helpful in making your life less demanding and more grounded.

Short-Circuiting Guilt Trips

At times even without meaning to, parents push guilt on their children when they feel excluded or dismissed.

"When I call," says Rose, an overworked physician with a child, "my mother repeats 'Who is this?' or 'Who did you say is calling?' several times, acting as if she doesn't know. That really turns up the guilt a few notches."

Some parents pretend that it is really okay that you are too busy for them. Laura's mother often tells her, "I know you're busy. You're young, you have your own life to live; don't worry about me." Laura finds it impossible to take her mother's words at face value. "I hear in her voice the dejection of being cut off when I can't linger on the telephone to give her every detail of a dinner I've eaten at a new restaurant or of meeting my son's new girlfriend. That tone—the hesitancy of wanting to know more, to talk longer—resounds in my ears. I hear it long after I've hung up. Quickly, and every time, the short shrift I've doled out turns into guilt."

If a parent has an uncanny knack for calling at the wrong time, these repeated and unnecessary interruptions can undermine your desire to stay in touch. Sophia recognizes that her mother is needy, but "there are times she just wants to talk. Those times are never on my schedule. If I call her with a question and she doesn't feel like chatting, she says, 'Gotta go,' but when I say that, she gets bent out of shape."

Obligatory calls, rushed calls, and intrusive calls tend to lead to hurt feelings, even if you apologize, explaining that you're late for an important meeting, your workout, car pool, a promising date, or your child's Little League practice. Your parents may say they understand, but you still feel that familiar pang of guilt . . . again. Instead, eliminate repeated and inconvenient phone calls by

- requesting that your parent call you at home or work—whichever is likely to be less chaotic.

- telling your parents when *not* to call you—at dinnertime, during the children's bathtime, not before 8 P.M., not after 10 P.M.
- offering to call them at a specific time that's more convenient—and less pressured—for you. Then be sure to do so.
- agreeing on the number of times per week you will speak with each other.
- surprising them with a call just to say I love you, I miss you, or to tell them when something special happens.

Whether you talk in person or on the telephone, making realistic, manageable arrangements goes a long way in alleviating guilt and stress. Choose times that are convenient, and fix arrangements and agreements in advance. But let's be practical—there never seems to be quite enough time. If your schedule is such that you can't keep to a set time, be clear about that with your parents so they are not disappointed . . . and waiting. And if your schedule is too crowded for you to set up a predictable time, make sure your parents understand that, too. Explain your time conflicts and ask for their patience. Uncomplicated, factual statements keep the connection going when life interferes. But it's incumbent upon you to honor the commitment you make to your parents—failing to follow through or doing so in a haphazard manner will stretch your connection to the breaking point.

With good planning, there is enough of you to go around. Whatever the blueprint of your individual connections, by determining a specific time to chat with your parents and setting aside worries and distractions so that you can concentrate on the conversation, you are creating an environment that will be more satisfying to you both.

You Might Say

- I know you want to catch up.
- I want to hear what's going on in your life, too.
- By Sunday, I have to (list your commitments and obligations).
- I can't call you before (day or week).
- Please be patient.
- I love you and want to talk to you . . .
- . . . and will, as soon as I can.

Or You Might Say

- I'm crazy busy this month, but I want to see you.
- Why don't we agree to talk every Saturday morning?
- Next month, when pressures lighten up, we'll go out for breakfast.
- Or, we can meet for dinner on Wednesday night.
- Let's make a firm date.

The Frequency Factor

Staying connected has entirely different connotations within families, and the frequency of contact depends on personalities and your and your parents' expectations for the relationship. Some adult children and parents speak daily; others, weekly or monthly. For many, the content of the contact is irrelevant. Rebecca and her mother speak at least four times a day on the telephone. "About nothing," chortles Rebecca. "My husband can't understand how two people can talk for hours about absolutely nothing."

Some people can be in touch less often and pick up right where they left off. Ross hasn't seen his mother in four years because she won't fly, and he has been sailing the world as a ship captain. He and his father cross paths several times a year when his father travels for business. Ross describes his relationship with his parents as close. He speaks to his mother every two weeks and e-mails once a week. E-mail and instant messaging effectively compensate for large periods of time between visits in person.

Frequency becomes a more serious issue if a parent measures love and loyalty by how often you call or if he or she has a high "worry" index. In thirty-three years, Talia has become well aware of her mother's scorekeeping, so she tries to call every week but is not consistent. Her mother waits for the call and rarely calls her daughter. "With my mother, the more we talk, the better our relationship is. Now that I'm a mother, we have a lot more in common and can chat forever. She wants to hear about her granddaughter, and that can be a half-hour conversation. We e-mail a lot, which keeps the contact tight and helps keep me on her good list."

There's no scorekeeping between Fran and her mother, who both lead busy lives. Fran's mother is a school principal who writes children's books. She recently married a man with young children, so her free time is even more restricted. Fran, a twenty-seven-year-old law student from Austin, Texas, is just as busy dividing her time between studying, working to pay for her education, and having a social life with her boyfriend. "My mother and I respect each other's commitments and have a quietly understood closeness without speaking to each other on a regular basis," explains Fran. "We don't get annoyed when we can't talk, so the pressure many of my friends feel to talk every other day or get together at set times isn't there. My mother is never demanding of my time, and vice versa. I think she likes it that way," Fran says, laughing.

For the majority of people, more consistent contact fortifies bonds and satisfies their needs to express love, lessen concern, feel validated, or simply keep current on family matters. Although married with a baby and a hectic job, Michael goes out of his way to be sure his mother knows he loves her. He calls once a week, tells her he loves her, and sends flowers for Mother's Day, Thanksgiving, and Christmas. Michael is always willing to listen to the latest news about what his mother's friends are doing so she understands that he cares.

Kathrine lives alone in a large city and has a different, sensible approach for staying connected to her parents. Although she talks to her mother—who is good at putting things in perspective—every day or two about day-to-day frustrations, regular contact assures Kathrine that her parents are available should she need them. "Knowing my parents are there for me is really important. If anything bad ever happened, I'm confident they would drop everything to be with me, and I wouldn't have to ask them. I count on them, and they know I count on them, a lot, but they like that."

Beverly, a fifty-five-year-old telephone company executive, has a more philosophical and historically based rationale for keeping her connection strong—one she maintains during lengthy Sunday telephone calls. "My mother is really the person most interested in me and what I'm doing. My sister and I are her life. Really, who else cares that much about your well-being or your children? My father would too, I'm sure, if he were alive. Who else wouldn't miss a graduation or a milestone celebration? I can't think of anyone, and that includes my husband and children, who cares about me more than my mother. My life is scattered, but my mother is a constant. Our phone conversations are essential to her, but they are also essential to me."

OPTIONS FOR SMOOTHER CONNECTIONS

- Determine how much time you are willing to give your parent.
- Clarify your time restraints, if you have any.
- Schedule prearranged phone calls and/or visits.
- E-mail consistently to fill in holes between calls and visits.
- Set up instant messaging on your and your parents' computers.
- Offer extra time when you have it.

The Near or Far Dilemma

Adult children are split in their opinion about the value of proximity in staying connected to their parents. Some find distance helpful; others find the separation created by distance detrimental to their bond. Where you fall on the distance continuum affects how you communicate with your parents.

Carolyn, forty-four, and her husband of fifteen years live about four miles from her parents. Carolyn is attached to her mother and relies on her for baby-sitting, something her mother can't do on a regular basis for Carolyn's sister, who lives five hundred miles away. "I know my sister misses my mother and we all realize my mother's being available to help me is one of the things that keeps us so connected."

While Carolyn's mother is helpful and supportive, Lacey's mother, who also lives nearby, is demanding. Lacey feels her mother's emotional dependency is fed by Lacey's accessibility. "I would like my mother to be self-sufficient. She expects me to be there for her on a daily basis, to call her, to stop in. She's perfectly fit; she needs no help. Mind you, she's only sixty-four."

In contrast, Roberta lives hundreds of miles from her parents, a distance that, according to Roberta, prevents constant conflict and disappointment. Roberta is highly efficient and compulsive, the opposite of her mother, a personality difference that aggravates Roberta. "I have really high expectations of my mother, and any time she doesn't do exactly what she says—which is most of the time—I freak out. It's been very healthy for our relationship to live far apart."

The effect of proximity on your relationship, like the frequency of contact, depends greatly on your emotional makeup and willingness to work on the relationship. Jocelyn's adult relationship with her mother is a mirror to the one she had with her mother as a child. "If something's bothering me, I tell her. When I was in college she drove up to visit much more than the other parents. My mother loves my kids and loves to be with them. We make an effort to be together—we go to dinner, just the two of us, we shop. I can't imagine not having her near me. I know when they move, I'll be devastated."

Those who live apart find ways to close the distance. To Cara, the forty-five miles that separates her from her mother seems too far until she realizes that if her mother were around the corner, as much as she would enjoy that, it would create a different kind of tension. Cara thinks she would probably spend more time with her mother than she would with her husband. To make up for the time they are apart, Cara and her mother vacation two weeks a year in a small cabin, just the two of them.

If you live a great distance from your parents, you may feel the absence more sharply when you have children or when you or your parents have a problem. Delia makes a strong case for being near your parents in both good and bad times. "It never occurred to me that having children would deepen my bond with my mother. But when I became a mother, I really started missing being with my mother. I want to keep telling her what the kids say and do. I want her to experience them. She loves the boys so much; the distance is such a problem."

Delia lives 900 miles from her parents. Her marriage is disintegrating, and she is thinking of moving closer to them because she could use her family's support. She knows she could go home tomorrow, and there would be a place for her and the children. But she also admits that "many things about my life I can't tell my parents. Maybe I'm better off where I am."

Turning Estranged Relationships Around

When the connection between parent and adult child is good, most problems can usually be remedied, but reestablishing the connection when the relationship is strained or estranged takes hard work and commitment to reconnect. Good communication helps strengthen good or acceptable bonds, but is vital in a relationship with a grudge-holding parent who is speaking to you one day, not speaking to you the next, for a relationship that exists with personal attacks and provocation, and for one that has gone long stretches of time without contact.

The longer the stretch of time without contact, the more difficult it is to get back on track, regardless of the severity or silliness that caused the break originally. As a first step in sorting out conflict, consider sending an E-mail or letter to get your parent's attention. It took Christina six months to learn why her mother refused to speak to her. After five months of no contact, she sent a letter stating that she and her mother had to work it out. Another month passed before her mother responded. The meeting, set for a neutral spot, was not particularly pleasant, but it unlocked the door to mending what turned out to be her mother's placing blame on Christina for knocking over the Christmas tree when in fact the tree stand had been broken. Her mother knew about the broken stand, but was too headstrong to apologize. Christina, who has had years of experience with her mother's stubbornness, chose to persist until she got the relationship back on speaking terms.

Connections and peace can also be restored if you are willing to be receptive to gestures of reconciliation from a parent. Morgan and her father reached the point at which they could not speak to each other without one or both of them becoming enraged to such an extent that a reasonable conversation was out of the question. The last tirade was over a car Morgan wanted to buy. She finally resorted to a written ultimatum: She told her father to stop treating her badly, or they could not have a relationship.

A few weeks after Morgan's warning arrived, her father

flew from New Jersey to Oregon to spend the weekend with his daughter. It was the first time they had been together for any significant amount of time, and although it was tense, they talked the whole weekend and got through it without an argument. Morgan describes the weekend as "the beginning of something new. Knowing my father was interested in making the relationship better gave me self-confidence to want to do the same. We still have angry exchanges, but now I say, 'Daddy, instead of saying what would make me angry, why not say . . . ,' and he takes my suggestion. It took a long time, but we turned the relationship in a positive direction."

Learning to harness unpleasant exchanges immediately so that they don't escalate was the key to making Morgan's relationship with her father a much happier one. Another strategy you may find helpful for repairing a relationship strain is to stop a conversation as it begins to heat up by explaining that you want to talk about "this" later, if you are with your parent, or you'll call back after you have calmed down, if you are on the telephone. Don't let too much time pass before calling back, and be prepared either to apologize or to begin again with a more rational approach or an agreement to drop the subject.

Devastating or unusual circumstances can trigger your need to open up in new ways that have a lasting impact on the relationship. Lucy, thirty-nine, moved away from home at the age of sixteen when she and her mother were fighting so badly they could not be in the same room together. Twelve years later Lucy returned home after a destructive marriage. "My heart was broken. That's when my relationship with my mother really began. She helped me through my despair. I lay my head on her lap, and she soothed me, made me feel really good. From then on, whenever I have problems or am very upset, I call her, and she always has the right words. She soothes my heart."

Keeping Everyone Happy

When you are in a committed relationship, it's no longer just you trying to find time to talk or be with your parents. You must also consider your partner and his relatives, as well as your children and what works for them as part of the mix. You wind up with more arrangements to make and more people whose feelings might be hurt—quite easily. At the same time you become more rigid about your time, be it on the telephone or at family get-togethers. Both conversations and visits shrink because of family obligations on two sides. Your spouse's parents, for instance, want to see you and the children as much as your parents do.

Warning parents in advance of what you hope to accomplish on a given weekend day or holiday and spelling out how long you will be with them softens the blow of having to share you and of watching you pack up the children to race to the in-laws' or a friend's home. Clear explanations ahead of a get-together usually make limited time and hasty departures more acceptable.

All the explaining in the world will not totally eliminate disappointments and jealousy, but candidly acknowledging feelings makes it easier to deal with them. Elizabeth's mother is sure her daughter spends more time with her in-laws than with her and her husband. "My mother puts a lot of guilt on me if we don't see my parents enough. Fortunately, she recognizes that she does this, and that makes it possible for me to talk to her about it."

Now, though, Elizabeth says she and her husband are planning to move, but closer to which family is a complicated and troubling question. They have strong relationships with both families and want to spend time with each of them, but both sets of parents live out of state in different directions. When Elizabeth told her parents that they were likely to move closer to her in-laws, her mother did not deal with the news very well. "When we talk about the whole moving situation, I get angry, probably unnecessarily so, but I do," admits Elizabeth. "I understand; putting myself in her situation, I would feel the same way. It's hard for me as well, but she makes me feel more conflicted, instead of realizing I have to do what's best for my family."

Holidays are particularly stressful if your parents offer no options. Some parents feel it is their right to have their children and grandchildren at the holiday table. Neither fifty-year-old Richard nor any of his five brothers and sisters would dream of missing holiday dinners. They know they are expected to show up, that certain holidays are important to their mother. "My mother should have been Jewish; she has Jewish guilt so down pat she could be teaching it to Jewish mothers," Richard jokes. "I can't conceive of not being home for Thanksgiving or Christmas. Even to my siblings who are divorced and have children and a mess of holiday obligations, my mother announces, 'I have Thanksgiving on Thursday at five o'clock. You make arrangements, and you show up at five with the kids.'" She makes life difficult by not acknowledging that her grandchildren should spend some holidays with their other parent or grandparents.

Holidays aren't the only instances when face time with parents can be a big issue; if you live fairly close to your parents, you could experience a regular tug-of-war over who goes to visit whom on ordinary days or weekends. Sally and her husband find it easier to show up at her parents' house than to argue. "We visit often for dinner, to watch a video, or to sleep over. My father likes to stay home; it's his kingdom, and he wants his children to flock around him. A lot of the relationship is us going to them." Sally sighs resolutely. "Fortunately my husband understands my father and is agreeable and supportive of my relationship with my parents."

When the person you share your life with is not supportive or displays outright disdain for your parents, arranging to see them can be near impossible, and actual visits can be tense and terribly unpleasant. A partner's negative attitude in any form—be it resenting the time you spend with your parents or behaving in ways perhaps only you recognize as judgmental or ornery—makes remaining connected all the more difficult. Ellen and her husband live in a large city about an hour from Ellen's parents, but they visit only four or five times a year. Her husband doesn't want to make the effort or spend the money to rent a car, but most significantly, he's not particularly close to her parents and doesn't care whether or not they see them.

In such situations, you must take a stand, no matter how impossible, contrary, or indifferent your partner acts. Some partners "book" so much time with their own parents that there is little or none left for yours. Having a partner or spouse try to interfere with or obstruct your relationship with your parents will weaken, and eventually might even destroy, your parent-child bond. If attempts to ease the situation or to turn your partner around fail, make independent arrangements to speak or be with your parents: call your parents from work, take a trip alone to visit them; plan an afternoon at their home, perhaps to work on a mutual project, if they live close enough to you; or arrange to take a getaway weekend together.

Tidbits of your parents' past or interesting glimpses of what they are like inject a heightened sense of camaraderie and understanding into your bond if you take the time to talk to your parents.

Well past age forty, Sophia started asking questions of her father, only to learn how much alike they were both in idiosyncratic ways and in areas that affected her life as a child and in her functioning as an adult. Unbeknownst to each other before Sophia probed, they both nap on their office floors, a likeness they find amusing. When Sophia was a child, her father moved from job to job, and the family from place to place, for reasons that had never been fully explained to her. When her father divulged his diagnosis of attention deficit disorder (ADD), the job losses not only made sense but also became a link between them—Sophia too has a mild form of ADD.

When you stay connected with your parents, you may discover explanations for important events and circumstances in your families. You may also come to see your parents as people, not just as the parents you had when you were growing up.

How to Make Time Together More Comfortable

- Being the initiator gives you more control over time and place.
- If you decide the time and place, you will feel less confined, allowing you to be open to suggestions from your parents.
- To avoid problem topics, decide what you want to discuss before you make contact.
- It's perfectly okay to withhold information—you're an adult.
- Don't allow a partner to block your relationship with your parents.
- Spend time alone with a parent—even a few minutes—without your partner or children.
- Listen when your parents talk; they need to feel they play a role in your life.
- Before plunging into an argument, ask yourself if it's worth it.
- Say "I love you" as often as you can.

FOUR

Drawing Boundaries

As important as it is to stay connected to your parents, it's equally imperative to have boundaries. Parent-child relationships teem with pushing and pulling—much of which lingers in adulthood. Parental intimacy, encouragement, nurturing, and support—crucial while you were growing up—can be a beneficial part of adulthood, but can also feel smothering when parents don't respect your separateness.

It's far too common to have a parent who wants to make decisions for you or attempts to live out his life through you. Such a parent may feel it his duty to tell his child what he should or should not be doing. Or the parent may be unable to see how tightly her life and yours are intertwined. Parents like this have emotional needs so great that they can only be met if the adult child sacrifices her identity and literally melds it into her parent's. Tanya, for example, married the man her mother chose and gave up her own dreams to satisfy her mother. "I had no will of my own," she says, "because I risked losing my mother's love if I did." After several years of marital anguish, Tanya divorced, separated herself from her mother's excessive involvement, and at the age of thirty-five finally regained her sense of self.

Roxanne is thirty-seven and continues the struggle. "My mother thinks I'm a part of her, like an arm or a leg; I wish she wouldn't criticize me as if she were looking in a mirror, criticizing herself. She doesn't know the power of her words. I wish she'd remember that I'm a separate person. When I'm older, I'm going to make an effort not to live through my child."

Before casting all blame on your parents, entertain the idea that you, too, may be at the root of the entanglements. Lucas, thirty-five and a weather forecaster, accepts partial responsibility for being entwined, but he wants his boundaries marked and observed: "It may be that I don't know how to relate to them except as their child. It's a delicate balance, and that's probably connected to why I want to keep them out of many areas of my life as I try to assert myself and see myself as an adult."

Ten years ago Lucas went to great lengths to change the patterns that defined his relationship with his parents—he felt nagged and judged at every turn. At age twenty-five he left Cleveland and moved to Houston because his parents infringed on the adult parts of his life. Living in a different city gave Lucas a buffer zone so he's not bombarded with unwanted attention. By being somewhere else, with no prior expectations to fill, no preordained path to follow, he has made his life easier. He talks to his parents weekly. Conversations that used to be awkward have become comfortable and more affectionate. Intrusive calls his parents viewed as supportive and Lucas viewed as a nuisance have stopped.

If you have a push-pull dichotomy in your relationship, keeping boundaries clear will be more difficult but is worth the effort. Devin, who has a mixture of love and loathing for her mother, has been able to avoid her mother for a year at a time if she chooses. But, Devin points out, "If I had a terrible problem or if I were very sick, I wouldn't go to anyone else. She's the only person I can talk to. She's the only person I know I can call in the middle of the night, and she would drive to wherever I am. I've realized this and am at the point where I'm trying to rebuild the relationship without getting stuck in her web."

Subconscious ties to parents are much more obscure and complex to identify and assess. Buried quite deeply in the back of your mind may be the notion of your parents as a safety net—a rescue team to bail you out, regardless of your adult status or, like Devin, the extent of the difficulties in the relationship. You assume you are independent until a crisis develops and you need your parents. It's wonderful to have parents to rely on, as long as turning to them does not develop into a habit that impedes your independence or keeps the relationship from moving in a balanced direction.

Marcia got divorced at thirty-eight and her father, a recent widower, invited her to live with him. "Convenient, safe, easy" were the words that rushed into Marcia's mind in her frazzled and confused state—a refuge, a haven from all she was going through. Sharing his home would have solved many of her immediate problems, but she was aware of the dependency issues, the reporting in, the responsibility of cooking, and so much more. Within minutes Marcia came to her senses—living with her father, even temporarily, was retreating to being taken care of, a loss of ground. "I said, 'Thanks, Dad, but you and I would last maybe four days together in the same house.' I love my dad, but we needed to be apart. We both had to relearn how to survive by ourselves."

Defining Boundaries

If your parents have difficulty accepting your independence and the fact that they do not control your life, you need to draw lines your parents may not cross. You can define boundaries in different ways: Straightforward explanations satisfy some parents; others need stronger declarations from their adult children.

When boundaries are blurred or nonexistent, the first step in establishing them is to think through what you will or will not do and then state that in plain terms to your parents. Not only does a pronouncement clarify the rules of your interactions, but it also helps you feel less like your parents' pawn.

Sharon's parents never adapted to the reality that she's a grown woman, forty-one and approaching middle age. They're amazed she bought a house without their input and have a persistent worry that something's going to happen to her—a "woman alone" kind of concern, Sharon calls it. "I remind them I lived in Montana for five years and carried a gun, for God's sake, but they worry when I get on a plane or take a trip. They want me to call them when I arrive, and when I return home. I told them quite firmly, 'I love you, but I'm not calling.' I call them a couple of days after I get home." Sharon felt her parents infiltrated her boundaries by asking her to check in; while it may not have been an unreasonable request, it was one Sharon felt she had to ignore to keep her boundaries comfortable.

In subtle ways, Faith's mother monitored her life even though they hadn't lived in the same city since Faith graduated from college. Faith's mother was her consultant on how to dress, how to wear her hair, and who her friends should be. All suggestions were offered not as advice but with the comment, "But you do what you want. It's your life." Faith recalls that "every time my company moved me to a different city, my mother arrived to help me buy what I needed, arrange the furniture, and settle me in, put food in the refrigerator, that sort of thing. My last move was to San Francisco, and she couldn't get here."

When Faith's mother did visit, she might have been compensating for not being able to help Faith move in, but she was extremely critical of everything. "My mother told me she thought the couch might look better under the window. And didn't I think the kitchen needed a coat of fresh paint? I didn't say anything until she told me I had put the drinking glasses in an inconvenient place. I felt like one of those cartoon characters with a bolt of lightning zapping its head." Her comments were too invasive for Faith to overlook. "Through gritted teeth I simply said, 'Mother, this is my home. I like the glasses on that shelf, and no, I don't think the couch needs to be moved.' Since I normally don't speak to her that way, she heard me telling her to stop interfering in my decisions." Faith put her mother on notice to respect her new boundaries.

When innuendos, edicts, or honest explanations don't work, you may have to be brutally blunt and very specific. This is especially true if parents invade your personal space in inappropriate ways. Molly's mother questions her about her sex life, and Molly thinks it's not any of her mother's business. If there's no man in Molly's life, her mother jokes and makes disgusting, crude remarks. She pays no attention to her daughter's boundaries. Molly needs to tell her mother that such conversations make her uncomfortable and that her private life is off-limits—no more questions, no answers.

Inappropriate interference was not new to Nicole, whose family controlled her life from an early age. Marriage, divorce, and distance made no difference in her family's intrusion into her life, and Nicole was quite disturbed that her family wanted to know everything—from what medication she took to whom she was dating. If her mother wasn't asking, someone else in the family was— her stepfather, her aunt, or her grandfather—forcing Nicole to take a rigid stance. "I finally told my family, 'This is it; I'm an adult, I'm thirty-two. Whether or not you like the way my life is, I need you to stay out of it.'"

Changing Patterns

Establishing boundaries clearly and verbally is the first step toward gaining an independent life, which will ultimately improve how you and your parents interact. You may have to modify old patterns etched into the relationship over years and decades of being together, too. About to turn fifty, Diane became determined to change the way she related to her mother. For most of her forty-nine years, she tried to judge what mood her mother was in and approach her accordingly. Then Diane decided to stop tiptoeing around her mother. When her mother told her that her house was too small, the kitchen needed redoing, and she needed to add some plantings in the front yard, rather than allow her mother to denigrate her house constantly, Diane responded with, "I understand you don't like the house, but we like the neighborhood, and the house hasn't stopped us from having fun.' She thinks before she speaks now." Being outspoken helped Diane alter other patterned behavior. "When she complains that I don't call her, I tell her I've been too busy, but she could have called us."

Saying what's on your mind keeps your parents from having to guess, and, more importantly, gives them the opportunity to amend inconsiderate or manipulative behavior. Speaking up is more difficult to do, however, if you have a long history of being "obedient." Dorianne, for example, was a shy child with an outgoing mother who decided what her daughter could do and what opinions she should have. Her mother literally talked for her when they were in social situations. Dorianne saw herself as a model child, and a closeness developed because she felt so dependent on both parents, and they became dependent on her devotion to them. When Dorianne married Scott, she found her voice and was not as needy with her parents.

"When they visit, my mother takes over in a hyperorganized way," explains Dorianne. "She orders my father to hang the pictures, move this chair here, take out the garbage, whatever. She straightens up papers and tells me to straighten up the kitchen or living room. Now I tell her to chill out, this is my house. I'm not the submissive child I was. They want to see me more than I want to see them, but I feel comfortable saying they can't visit on a particular weekend, Scott and I have plans."

The word *no* is a freeing agent and changes unproductive patterns of relating. You may have to get over being afraid to set limits or to tell a parent you are angry. Saying how you feel is more effective than blowing up or suppressing your discomfort. Most relationships with parents, built on decades of love and respect, are deeper than the difficulties and survive the switch to new, more relaxed ways of being together. Lillian, thirty, and her father were locked in conflict over her being single. Her father's marriage expectations for her were grating, and about the only thing they talked about. Her father thought marriage and children were the only way to go; he told her she was going to be sorry later on if she didn't get married. If she told him she was happy with her career as a pharmaceutical company representative and traveling, he said she was wrong and was making a mistake. He knew that Lillian was open to marriage someday, but he wanted to know when. Eventually Lillian put an end to the habitual conversation. "I told him I'm not getting married and having kids just to get him off my back. He's been forced to find less personal and sensitive subjects to discuss."

Just because parents raised you doesn't mean you have to put up with continued demoralizing, selfish, or insensitive behavior. You always have a choice in how you interact with your parents. Alan's father often said hurtful things to him or to Alan's wife about him. Friends told him to write off his father; instead, Alan discovered a way to maintain a connection—in fact, a pleasant ritual, by Alan's account—that keeps him in regular contact without leaving much room for his father to diminish him. Alan limits his time with his father to ensure the time together is rewarding for both of them. "I've included my father in my Thursday-night poker game. It's a friendly game, and the other men find Dad charming and amusing. He sees me once a week, has dinner with the guys, plays a couple hours of poker, and I drive him home. He's one of the boys for the evening, and I admit I, too, think he's a great guy in that controlled setting."

Alan made an honest appraisal of the relationship and came up with a plan, a compromise that allowed him routine contact that both he and his father enjoy. Best of all, Alan chose to put his negative feelings aside. As Alan notes, "I don't feel guilty about ignoring or avoiding him as I had done in the past."

With boundary aids securely in place or ready to call into action if required, you can safely untie the apron strings and avoid slipping into old traps and patterns that can keep you deferring to parents as if you were still a child.

CHECKLIST FOR DRAWING BOUNDARIES

- Let a parent know when he or she exceeds your boundaries.
- Educate parents with explanations of your feelings.
- State that you don't feel comfortable doing or talking about what they ask.
- Answer questions with responses that offer limited information.
- Demonstrate by example, using stories of incidents with friends.
- Introduce the concept of privacy in small increments.
- Clarify that visits need to be planned.
- Handle a situation yourself rather than asking your parents.
- Look for a compromise that will reduce your stress.
- Add the word *no* to your vocabulary.

Who's the Parent?

The same strong feelings of love, devotion, and obligation that cause parents to hold on to their adult children prompt adult children to be too involved in their parents' lives—too concerned about a parent's well-being, too protective, or too in charge. Behaviors like these are often left over from years of worrying about a parent's emotional state or bailing out a parent from difficult situations. If you have an expanded sense of obligation, it could have started during a period of a conflict or crisis—a divorce, illness, or death—and remained in place too long.

Adult children who come from homes with substance abuse or chronic illness frequently become "parents" at an early age and continue in that role as grown-ups. Being excessively involved can turn you into your parents' parent. You may find yourself telling your parent to get help for her drinking problem, negotiating problems between your parents, being a stand-in spouse, or making simple everyday arrangements and plans when you shouldn't be. You run the risk of parenting your parents when there is no real reason to do so and infringing on your parents' autonomy.

In Tina's family there's no confusion about parenting status. Tina knows she is the parent. She would prefer it be otherwise, but can't release herself as acting marriage counselor and detail person for her parents. "My father's behavior during their marriage was reprehensible, but my mother wasn't mature enough to get help without me insisting. I have this reputation among my siblings as the one who has to tell everybody how it is.

"I'm the planner and organizer. If my parents need plane tickets, I buy them and send them. My mother, in particular, acts as if she can't figure out how to get from here to there. It's trivial stuff, but I feel as if I've been doing it for my parents my whole life. I'm the one who's responsible. It's partly my own doing, but it's also because my parents look to me."

Roberta has felt like her parents' parent for as long as she can remember, but unlike Tina, she not only realizes she should back off, but also does something about it. Roberta believes her parents seriously lack life skills, and when they divorced, she worried that she would have to take care of both of them because they had always seemed very helpless and scattered. Soon after the divorce, her father met someone, and Roberta was relieved, but her mother was overwhelmed, fearful, and continued to be impractical. Her mother was supposedly helping Roberta plan her wedding, but she made the process harder. If they had an appointment with a florist or caterer, Roberta went without her mother, who could be counted on to be late. On more than one occasion, her mother arrived an hour after the set time with no money to pay for the cab ride she'd taken to get there. Roberta, to counter what she perceived to be a lack of common sense, became reserved in the amount of assistance she provided. "I try to step back; I put more time between our visits together and decide when *not* to help her," she says.

As much as Roberta tries to remove herself from her watchdog role, Stephanie dives into a take-charge mode at full throttle. She confesses to having a constant need to take care of her parents, and she has been helping her parents make decisions for years. She supports them in times of family crisis as well as assuming some of their financial burdens.

When her grandmother died, Stephanie, found the

necessary papers and made the funeral arrangements. "I did everything; then it dawned on me: I'm the grand-daughter. My mother was appreciative, but admitted she would have done it if I hadn't been there." In other aspects of their lives, Stephanie feels her parents are not able to manage alone, so she consciously seeks ways to help. "I always seem to make life easier for my parents."

It is important to be sensitive to your parents'—and your own—potential discomfort with so much help. Stephanie was happy to feel grown up, but assistance may not always have such a pleasant effect on parents. Your parents may feel childlike and insecure if you come to their aid prematurely. And providing too much assistance can color your feelings toward them, as Stephanie eventually concluded. "I'm finally getting angry. Maybe it's because my company is not doing well right now, or because I'm realizing parents make decisions in their own lives that shouldn't have anything to do with their children—like buying a house they can't really afford. As the child and an adult, I don't need to feel so responsible for their poor decisions. After helping my mother find a job, helping with the house payments, and countless other things, I'm wondering if I'm being too much the parent here. They're not fragile old people. I'm sure if there's such a thing as a past life, my parents were my children."

Adult children, like Stephanie, who have had more education and hold high-income jobs often display role reversal earlier. Unlike her immigrant parents, Inge graduated from college and is president of a major catalog company. Because of her education and life experiences, Inge handles all her parents' practical matters—car or health insurance, retirement plans, or any type of investing. Her parents get confused and don't know what to do and have been looking to Inge since her first job. "At a young age I took over these things; I do a lot for my parents now because they did so much for me when I was growing up." When you are supportive, be cautious, or at least be aware of the issues your "parenting" may raise in your parents, making sure you don't violate their boundaries or yours.

EMOTIONALLY DEPENDENT PARENTS

Inge volunteers guidance gladly without coercion from her parents, but some parents pressure their adult children to act as their parents not only in practical matters but also in the psychological realm. Due to her mother's periodic depression, Karen feels her mother expects her to be her emotional caretaker. Her mother's depression-related neediness and instability is a disappointment to and a drain on Karen. She has tremendous respect for her mother and thinks she did an incredible job raising her, her sisters, and her brother, but Karen finds her mother hard to be around. "When I'm with her, she wants to mimic me—whatever shoes or clothes I'm wearing, she wants. Anything I do is perfect in her eyes, which drives me nuts. I've wanted to look up to her as a mother, but more often she looks to me for conversation, for guidance, for a lot of things."

An emotionally dependent parent can turn you into a full-time, all-purpose crutch if you allow it, and the repercussions can be grave. Natalie became the referee during her parents' stormy marriage and found herself responsible for her mother's emotional and financial needs when the family business started to fail. For five years Natalie was the family's savior, a period during which her father didn't want to deal with anything having to do with her mother, the house (although he lived there), or his failing printing business. Natalie had to fend off creditors, make sure her mother had money in her pocket, and try to restrain her parents during violent marital outbursts. The strain of being the grown-up for her parents culminated in her prolonged drug use and a subsequent series of bad relationships. Natalie looks back at the personal boundaries she didn't draw: "I should have refused to assume so much of my parents' burdens. My stepsiblings were much smarter; they had walked away years before."

Your emotionally stable parent can turn up the pressure, too, acting dependent when things don't go as smoothly as hoped or planned. During those times, you may find yourself in stressful, accommodating positions without intending or wanting to be there. Even when your intentions are good, you may be diminishing a parent's self-esteem and independence though at first your support seems constructive and necessary. The predicament then is how to stop what has become routine and expected.

Olivia's father has not remarried and has not considered a relationship since his wife left him over two decades ago. He's sixty-nine years old, in excellent health and good shape, but a loner except for his daughter, on whom he increasingly relies to meet his practical and emotional needs. "I find myself making his doctor's appointments and buying his groceries," an embarrassed Olivia reports. "I've told him he can't call me every ten minutes to find out how to cook something or to tell me he's spilled bleach on his laundry. He's just looking for someone to talk to. I sometimes feel like a spouse substitute.

"My father needs to be proactive, not wait for me to give him ideas; not depend on me for getting out of the house. I've tried to encourage him to join the men's church group or to take a woman to the movies, but he's out of the habit of meeting and talking to people. It would be helpful if he took the initiative and not expect me to shoulder that, too. I'm a single mother with a child, a house, and a job. That's enough for one person."

You cannot force a parent to become more independent, but you can set boundaries if you are taking on too

---

GETTING UNSTUCK: QUESTIONS TO ASK YOURSELF

- Are you providing too much in the way of assistance? More than is essential?
- Are you treating your parent as less capable than he or she really is?
- Do you know how your parent feels about your support?
- Should your involvement be short-lived, to address and fix a particular problem quickly?
- Have *you* created a pattern that you need to modify or eliminate?
- Is your involvement with your parent disrupting your life? Your marriage?
- What changes can you make to gradually stop being so involved?
- Can you discuss your feelings with your parent?
- Can you share helping responsibilities with siblings, relatives, or close friends?
- Should your parent hire someone to help with certain responsibilities?

---

much responsibility or are too involved. Limit how much you are willing to do. Advise your parents on getting whatever assistance they may need, but you can not and should not shoulder all the responsibility for their emotional well-being.

FIVE

Your Partners, Spouses, and In-Laws

As soon as parents realize you are serious about some-one they become hopeful and nervous at the same time. Rarely is a potential mate welcomed unconditionally without some form of massive scrutiny and many questions from your parents. You may experience the same type of probing if you have a parent who is obsessed with seeing you married.

Peter's father worries that his divorce from Peter's mother has made his forty-two-year-old son marriage-shy. Peter interprets his father's comments as "a lot of suggestive selling rather than pressure. He'll mention my age and leaving a legacy—'If you're going to have children, you need to do it soon. You're not going find Miss Perfect, she doesn't exist; you're not Mr. Perfect.'" Peter acknowledges what his dad is saying, but is resolved not to put his life on a timeline to please his father.

Like Peter, Geneva is in no hurry to marry, a decision that may or may not be affected by her awareness of her father's infidelity. When her mother carps about Geneva being alone, the thirty-five-year-old reminds her mother that millions of people are married and still lonely, then tries to explain the difference between being alone and being lonely. When her mother launches into her "Why are you so afraid of commitment?" speech, which includes, "Not everyone cheats, look at your father," Geneva sits back and takes it. She can't tell her mother the truth.

Dina's parents handpicked a man for their recently divorced thirty-five-year-old daughter. "Anthony was their epitome of marriage material: a respected physician whose family my family has known for two generations. They didn't care that I wasn't passionately in love with him." They felt betrayed when Dina broke off the engagement.

When you find *your* Ms. or Mr. Right, your parents may feel that *no one* is quite good enough for their child. As soon as you introduce your parents to your potential life mate, objections and concerns pop into parents' heads—and out of their mouths. What your parents think and certainly what they say have immediate and long-term ramifications. When should you ignore their comments? How do you assert your feelings when faced with negativity about your relationship choice? And how do you resist the pressure to change your mind?

Pedigrees and charm, stability and decency, good values, or depth of feeling can easily get lost or overlooked in your parents' highly combustible and unpredictable reactions. Parents have insecurities that crop up when they feel threatened, especially by a child's intended spouse or partner. Someone who is smarter or prettier, more successful or more secure in his or her own skin, is someone a parent may avoid or attack. This kind of reaction generally has more to do with your parent's personality than with the person you bring home. Parents *may* be thrilled with your choice on sight because he or she looks like or reminds them of someone they love or loved, but they could as readily dislike them for the same reason. Parents' emotions and expectations collide when they meet the person you love.

I'd Like You to Meet . . .

Parents may handle the news that you're serious about someone rather badly—by saying nothing, by being stunned or difficult, or even by hiring private investigators to find hidden chinks in Prince Charming's armor. Where Daylle's parents usually had something to say about almost all of her decisions, they stayed silent about her fiancé except to say they wanted her to be happy. Daylle was disappointed that her parents did not validate her choice or tell her they liked the man she planned to marry. (It's a good bet that if your parents offer little encouragement or praise, they have strong reservations and in their withholding they are asking you to think over your decision because they are not happy with it.)

Your parents' disapproval may be voiced in a straightforward, blanket rejection that covers their unhappiness about everything or anything from the person's religion to shallow observations about looks and social status. Or, as happens often, your parents' reservations could just fall into the simple category of your mate's not being "good enough," a judgment having no foundation in reality whatsoever. In calculating a person's acceptance, your parent's egocentricity could also be a defining factor, one not easily discounted. Devin's father has specifics in mind for the man his daughter marries, and his wish list has a large measure of his own ego in it. Her father prefers quiet, passive guys for his daughter who don't seem to cause trouble, traits that closely match his own. While Devin scoffs at most of her father's preferences, she feels "a lot of pressure if my parents don't like someone and I do."

You may tell yourself not to take your parents' reactions to heart, but if you love and respect them, it's hard not to listen to what they say or imply by their silence. There are those, however, who are less swayed and less inclined to have their husband or wife satisfy their parents' criteria. Courtney's mother jumped on the faith and race difference when Courtney announced her marriage intentions. Her mother felt her future husband wouldn't be culturally sensitive to their family, and a few months before the wedding advised Courtney to think twice about the cultural disparity. Courtney was livid. "I have, and you better think twice before you say anything else," she told her mother. "I knew her next words were going to be about his ability to support me. I told her she either welcomed him or she would not be part of my life. She still doesn't really like him, but now that she sees how hard he's working, she's a bit more accepting of him."

The Underlying Issues

Most parents do try to accept the fact that their child's choice doesn't mesh with or come close to what they had in mind. They have to digest and absorb the differences and find answers to the questions they undoubtedly have: Will you be able to live comfortably? How will you deal with religious, race, and cultural differences? Social differences? Parents adjust slowly; they want proof, and how you address and answer the questions will affect their acceptance. Once your parents have good information or see how happy you are, they are more likely to feel comfortable, not only with your choices but also with the person you chose.

YOU'RE RAISING THE CHILDREN HOW!?

The wedding is the initial and obvious open arena for religious conflict. Margie was faced with in-laws who at first refused to attend their son's wedding if a priest officiated, the decision Margie, a Catholic, and her Jewish husband had made. "I saw marriage as a sacrament, a spiritual time, and my husband recognized that. I would not back down in spite of his parents' pressure for me to convert or to have a rabbi marry us. I wanted a marriage recognized by the church." Margie's in-laws came to her church wedding, which was the start of coping with their religious differences. To avoid conflict, Margie's husband didn't tell his parents when their grandson was baptized. For the most part, to satisfy both sides of the family, they partake in holidays celebrated by each of their religions.

If you decide to marry someone of a different faith or from a different culture, there's bound to be disagreement and disappointment, but compromise and openness can soothe what might otherwise be a rugged course. In order to keep both families happy, Amy (who is Jewish) and her fiancé (who is Japanese) had a priest and a rabbi officiate at the wedding ceremony and incorporated Jewish and Japanese wedding traditions. Her mother-in-law was saddened by their decision to raise the children in the Jewish faith, but she has been extremely supportive. Amy makes a point to thank her for attending Jewish rituals such her son's *bris* and is sensitive to her mother-in-law's feelings. "I'm pretty sure she's happy that her son is with someone who has a faith, but in her heart my Judaism is probably painful for her. I know she envisioned her son married to a Japanese woman. I had a long talk with her and asked her to let us know if anything is hard for her, to let us know if we can make something easier. My parents, who initially were so worried about the cultural differences, have said many times, if they could have handpicked my husband, they would have chosen him."

I LOVE TERRY

If you love someone of the same sex, parental acceptance can be hard-earned, and is often less related to the man or woman than to social stigma and your parents' limited understanding of gay life. Yet so many of the underlying issues and roadblocks—and ways to reassure or "win over" parents—are the same for heterosexuals and homosexuals. Many who have kept their sexual preference secret or changed their sexual identity after living as a heterosexual encounter resistance that softens with time and education.

Austin's parents had difficulty dealing with his same-sex relationship, but he told them, "This is me and I'm not going to change, and you let me know when you're ready so we can resume our relationship. Until then I'll be happy to send you birthday cards and talk on the phone every now and then, but don't expect me to come home on the holidays if my partner's not welcome.' I let them know I expected to spend holidays with Bob, and if he wasn't welcome in their home, I would be spending them with his family."

Austin suggested his parents meet Bob's parents, who shared a great deal in common with Austin's parents, so he was sure they would enjoy each other's company. It took several years before Austin's parents invited Bob into their home. Ever since then, he's been part of Austin's family.

Giselle, however, knew that she would have to make all the necessary accommodations related to maintaining her relationship with her parents because their fundamentalist Christianity was opposed to lesbianism. Giselle's parents have told her that she and Sheila, her partner of ten years, may visit, but they may not sleep in the same room. "You will act as if you're friends when we have guests," her father said. Giselle and Sheila have chosen to visit, but never spend the night at Giselle's parents' home. Although her parents truly like Sheila and enjoy spending time with the two women, the relationship is not as open as Giselle would like. Since she cannot bring Sheila to holiday dinners with her grandparents, she spends them with Sheila's family, but believes that once her grandparents die, she and Sheila will be able to join in all family celebrations and gatherings as a couple.

Judd had a different problem in gaining acceptance of his lifestyle choice and partner. His parents both grew up in small towns and had never been friends with or known any homosexuals. Judd is cautious about the people he allows his parents to meet because his parents are completely supportive in the abstract about his homosexual relationship, but when he tried to bring his partner into the family, his parents "acted weird, flipped out." His parents were very resistant and hypocritical—if Judd's brother Paul wants to include his girlfriend, he doesn't have to ask, he just brings her along. Judd mentioned their double standard to them, and they did an about-face, which "was so satisfying to me, given their provincial backgrounds."

After sixteen years of marriage and two children, forty-two-year-old Wyatt divorced his wife and moved in with Jack. His parents were emotionally and financially supportive of his breakup with his wife, but they didn't understand the life he chose, that he and Jack live like a heterosexual couple in a nice neighborhood. He learned that they were afraid to visit, associating homosexuality with pornography and a debauched lifestyle. They also worried that their son would get AIDS. "I'm not sure what else they pictured in their minds," says Wyatt, "but once I realized I hadn't taken time to teach them, I began to give them concrete examples and talked about our community service work and church activities. They became less fearful, and after they visited, they felt much better about Jack and my decision."

Natalie's mother has been accepting of Natalie's gay preference since she was in her twenties, but has always condemned any partner she's had. "I don't think her reaction is in any way related to my being a lesbian; she feels defenseless when there's another person in my life."

ADJUSTMENT PERIODS

Getting used to a new person, welcoming him or her, and ultimately accepting this person as part of the family takes time. Adjustment periods come with twists and turns as the relationship between your partner and your family and your partner and his family evolve to a satisfactory or better state. Compromises—large and small—bring good results.

Inge told her parents about her decision to marry her boyfriend before they had met him. Keith is older than her parents, so Inge was prepared for them to object to her decision not to have children because of Keith's age and the fact that he had grown children and grandchildren. She hoped they would understand how deeply she loved this man, but as Inge expected, her mother burst into tears and her father honed in on the age difference. Inge recounts her father's reaction: "'You're thirty-five, and you've never given me any trouble, so you either know what you're doing or you've completely lost your mind.' I gave them a few weeks to think about my news before asking them to meet Keith."

Inge's husband now goes out of his way to be supportive of her parents and includes them in family get-togethers with his children and grandchildren. Within a few months, her parents saw how extremely happy Inge was and were able to put the age factor aside and drop childbearing discussions.

However, some parents may cling to reservations that prevent them from wholly embracing your partner or spouse. Shortly after forty-four-year-old Heidi married her attorney husband, he decided he was not suited for the courtroom and made an economically downward career switch to teaching law. Seven years later Heidi's mother remains adamant that this is the worst decision in the world, and Heidi should divorce him. "I hear regularly how horrible this is and that we can't possibly survive on a teacher's salary," says Heidi. "Fortunately, my husband helped me see much of my mother's bizarreness, and when she starts on what she thinks is our poverty, I look at her and say, 'Get off it already. I married a person, not an income.'"

Following are calming approaches to use with parents who are upset or anxious about your choice in partner.

QUELLING UNDERLYING CONCERNS

- Assure your parents that your partner wants them to be part of your life together.
- Encourage acceptance by letting parents know when a partner or spouse acts in a loving or supportive way.
- Keep reminding your parents how much you love this person, how happy you are.
- Find common interests between your parents and your spouse or partner.
- Keep grating issues at bay.
- Maintain a close bond with your parents so they don't feel neglected or jealous of your partner or in-laws.

Surmounting In-Law Difficulties

Theoretically, your parents gain a son or daughter when you marry, but accompanying that belief, sincere or not when stated, is the sense that they are losing you. Parents fear—founded or unfounded—they will see less of you because available time gets parceled not only between spouse, children, and job, but also between two families—yours, and his or hers.

Pamela's future mother-in-law makes all the right gestures when trying to overcome the "loss" of her son, but Pamela does her part, too. Her mother-in-law buys Pamela gifts, asks to speak to her on the phone, and goes so far as to tell Pamela she's happy her son has found someone to love. Pamela responds to these overtures: "It's obvious she's jealous. I'm taking away her son; another woman is becoming important in his life. I give them lots of time alone so she doesn't feel threatened by me."

The issue of parents adjusting from having more of you to having less, from not having to share you to sharing you with others, has many permutations. If you defer to parents rather than accepting the natural progression of separate lives, you will add considerable stress to the partnership or marriage, and you may have to cope with the added complication of a parent who does not get along with your partner. Diligence in drawing parameters with such a parent will protect and keep the relationship with your parent feasible.

Daniel, who is thirty-eight and a new father, has a mother who always wants to be closer to him. She's the type of person who says, "I have to see you!" For most of Daniel's adult life he allowed his mother to drop in, but she and his wife barely tolerate each other. Although Daniel's mother wants to be in his home without restrictions, Daniel, needing to guard his marriage, has told her she can't be. Instead, he telephones her a couple of times a week; the calls make her feel as if she has ready access to her son. "She will have to get along with less of me than she's had in the past," Daniel says with conviction.

Living close to your in-laws can present a different set of privacy complications, particularly if your in-laws are helpful and generous. You can find yourself caught between wanting and needing in-law support and feeling invaded. Thea and her husband bought a "handyman special" that was in dire need of repair. Thea's father-in-law is retired and can do carpentry. First thing, he changed all the locks because he thought they weren't good. When Thea told him he should make keys for himself and her mother-in-law for emergencies, he told her he had already made them. Her in-laws worked on the house when she and her husband were at their jobs. Thea thought their behavior was creepy, but not worth fighting about, until she came home one evening after work and saw the porch light on and found dinner on the kitchen counter with a note.

"I thought, 'Okay, it's nice that they come over, fix stuff and leave us dinner. I need to concentrate on their thoughtfulness,' but then I looked around and noticed they had rearranged the living room furniture. I went upstairs to tell my husband I wish they would call to let us know they are coming over and see my mother-in-law's jacket on our bed. She and my father-in-law were repairing the windowsills in the bedroom. This kind of thing happens way too often," Thea says angrily.

Having her husband step in seemed the most logical solution. A son or daughter is the most likely candidate for requesting a change or calming the waters. You know your own parents better than your spouse does—you know their weaknesses and strengths, what lines can be crossed without creating mayhem, and when the emotional ice may be thin.

Monica needed her husband to intercede with her demanding mother-in-law on her behalf, but he wouldn't. "Our life is a soap opera, and she's the queen. If she doesn't have things her way, she whines," explains Monica, who got tired of being pushed around and has been telling her mother-in-law how she feels. "It may not be helping, but it makes me feel better."

If your spouse won't mediate during the early stages of tension and animosity, it will be impossible for him or her to be neutral when the situation comes to a head, when family members threaten not to speak to one another and everyone is forced to take a side. Cara's husband, Sam, was pushed into a corner when her in-laws, who thought she was adhering to Jewish customs, arrived unannounced in mid-December to find the house decorated for Christmas.

Cara defends her position. "I was thirty-nine, married for seven years, and very comfortable being a mutt, part Jewish, part Christian. When I converted to Judaism, I had to wipe out my background, and I willingly did, not for my in-laws but for the children we planned, but never had. I do Christmas because I grew up with Christmas. I have ornaments and decorations that have been in my family for many generations."

According to Sam, his parents started crying and going berserk. They said that Sam had to stop this, that Sam had to control Cara, but he refused. His father said, "You better, because if you don't, I'm never talking to you again." Cara's husband responded, "Fine, then you're never talking to me again."

A little later Cara called Sam's parents and explained that she didn't want to be cut off from the background and traditions she had grown up with, just like they never want to be cut off from theirs. Cara and her in-laws eventually agreed to disagree on religion, and Sam's parents agreed not to visit them in December. His parents know they throw holiday parties, but they never ask about them. The irony is that after their explosive beginning and middle, Cara adores her mother-in-law. "She's one of a handful of women I've met that I consider a role model."

Time changes many relationships with in-laws. Kenneth and his father-in-law got off to a rocky start. "He's still the classic, self-made entrepreneur, but he's not as ruthless as he was," comments Kenneth. "After I got over being intimidated by my father-in-law, we engaged in conversation.

We found out we had more in common than we'd ever imagined. I'm interested in business and banking and things that he's interested in. Much to our astonishment, I became his surrogate son, and he, my substitute father. We're the last people on the planet you'd ever put together, yet over the years he's become one of my favorite people."

It would be much more pleasant if sons and daughters and parents and in-laws accepted each other without gnawing reservations and a collective laundry list of doubts. Because parent's protective instincts are nearly impossible to extinguish, your best hope is that their worries will be proven wrong as everyone gets to know each other. Conceding, compromising, and laughing about dilemmas and individual quirks add harmony and make the important connections with parents and in-laws less burdensome.

IN-LAW RELATIONSHIP GUIDE

- Make concessions without sacrificing your values whenever you can.
- When the situation calls for it, take a firm position.
- If your partner can't set boundaries, you set them.
- Agree to disagree if you can't reach a satisfactory medium.
- Ask how you can help ease tensions.
- Take the time to address your in-laws' concerns.
- Be considerate and tolerant of an in-law's differing beliefs.
- Allow ample time for the kinks to work themselves out.
- Overlook the "small stuff" that upsets you.
- Be patient—relationships grow over time.

SIX

Your Parent's New Partner

Chances are that one or both of your parents will be with someone else at some point, if not already. Whether your parent has been widowed or divorced, your bond with the parent changes—sometimes temporarily, sometimes permanently. It's hard to welcome your parent's new partner amicably, especially if doubt about that partner's suitability holds you back.

When you question your parent's choice, he or she is torn between wanting to please you and retain the closeness you've always had and wanting to move on with his or her life. Parents seek acceptance and understanding from you in much the same way you seek approval for your mate choices.

If you haven't warmed to your parent's new arrangement or find it creates friction between you and your parent, figuring out the causes of your hesitation in accepting your parent's new partner should be your first step.

> ### POSSIBLE BARRIERS TO WELCOMING THE NEW PARTNER
>
> - You may have been watchful and protective of your parent—a watchfulness that borders on possessiveness—and are faced with the possibility of someone taking over your role.
> - Likewise, you could be dismayed that this new person is assuming the role of your much-loved deceased or absent parent.
> - You may perceive a new partner as open competition for your parent's time with you.
> - You may have difficulty thinking about your parent as a sexually active person.
> - If you thought your parent would remain alone, the change may make you anxious.

Puzzling Choices

When adult children don't embrace parents' new partners, they risk isolating themselves from their parents. Alexia found her mother's new significant other unacceptable. He had a sketchy background, couldn't hold a job, had his car repossessed, and alienated himself from everyone in the family with his vulgarity. Her mother didn't seem to mind and didn't make any effort to curb his impropriety.

Alexia tried to have a relationship with Gavin, but found him too crass. Her mother insisted they do things together, but Alexia refused. "My mother flew up from Georgia for my wedding, and for the first time in many years she said, 'It's okay for us to have a relationship that doesn't involve Gavin all the time.' That's what I needed to hear from the beginning," Alexia said.

You might be expected to be thrilled when your parent, especially an older one, finds happiness in remarriage or has someone special in her life after a divorce or the death of a spouse. But, it is seldom that simple. For five of the six years since Iris's mother died, Iris and her father have been at odds. As soon as her father began dating, forty-five-year-old Iris put divisive rules into place. "My father and this woman I loathe—I will not acknowledge her by mentioning her by name—spend Friday and Saturday together at my father's house. I insist that she pack up and leave by the time I arrive at eleven on Sunday mornings. I don't want her there when I am, and I don't want to see her toothbrush in the bathroom. I've told my father that if he marries her, he will never see me again. I haven't figured out why I have such strong feelings, but I'm working on it."

By holding fast to her initial negative impressions of her mother's third husband, Nicole creates ongoing tension among the three of them. Not letting go of her dislike makes her more miserable than it makes either her mother or stepfather. Nicole refers to her second stepfather as her mother's husband and describes him as stoic and dry in contrast to her mother's warm and bubbly nature. Nicole took immediate offense to his abruptness and the tone he used when speaking to her mother the first time she met him. Nicole jumped to her mother's defense, and in doing so put her mother in the middle of a struggle that has lasted more than a decade. Nicole cried through her mother's wedding ceremony, refused to pose for pictures, and followed that performance with one-sided phone contact for two years—telling her mother she would have to call Nicole, and that Nicole would never ask about the man her mother lives with.

Nicole's childlike behavior ended when she realized her attitude was detrimental to her own children. Her children think of her stepfather as Grandpa, and she doesn't want to jeopardize their relationship with him. "I'm merely a liaison, they're forced to include me. I like it when my mother's husband goes out of town; then I can stay there without feeling as if I'm intruding." The relationship with her stepfather remains awkward, but Nicole concedes her mother is content, and contrary to her original concern, her stepfather treats her mother well.

It can happen that your parent becomes involved with someone who, in contrast to Nicole's stepfather, has little interest in your children or you. Pamela's mother "found a man who is everything in her life," Pamela explains, "but he isolates himself from the rest of us by burying himself in a newspaper or book and mumbles only a few words when we try to bring him into the conversation. He doesn't seem to want to get to know us. Nonetheless, I always ask my mother how he's doing when I call and give her the impression that I think he's a wonderful person because I know she's happier than she's ever been."

In general, women have a harder time psychologically, socially, and financially after divorce; these are factors to consider when trying to comprehend a mother's new attachment. While fathers tend to fare better, particularly financially, their mate choices can be puzzling, too. Although you may be resistant and confused initially, when you step back, the reasons for and benefits of your parent's new connection usually become apparent, as Roberta discovered. Her dad divorced her mother to marry someone who is far less glamorous and more like his own mother.

Roberta's not crazy about her, but she sees she's better for him than her mother was. The new wife takes care of him, runs things for him. Roberta has a good relationship with her, and as Roberta points out, "we mostly get along well. It's not as if he ran off with somebody my age."

The appeal of younger women to older men confounds older women and disturbs sons and daughters when their own fathers pair off with younger women. Molly, a thirty-three-year-old horse trainer, admits her refusal to meet her father's much younger girlfriend is immature, but she can't imagine what her father sees in this woman. "When my dad tells me how wonderful she is and that she has an old soul," Molly says, laughing, "I ask him, 'Does that mean she knows Paul McCartney was in a band before Wings?' What can he possibly see in someone my age? We know what she sees in him—money."

You may have plausible reasons for disapproving of your parent's selection, but parents, like the rest of us,

---

WHEN YOU NEGATE A PARENT'S CHOICE OF A PARTNER, ASK YOURSELF

- What is the point of your behavior?
- What message are you sending, and why?
- How is your behavior affecting your parent and his or her relationship?
- How is your attitude affecting your parent's relationship with you?
- What do you hope to gain?
- Whom are you really punishing?
- Is your behavior going to change your parent's choice?

learn from their mistakes. "When my parents split up, my father introduced us to the woman with whom he had been having an affair," explains Tina. "She's mean-spirited, and that makes my sister and me sad. We'd like to see him move on and date people who'd give him more fulfillment, and we tell him so, but he likes the comfort he gets from her. He really knows that it's not a good relationship and that he should end it, but he can't. My father thought we didn't like her because she was the 'other woman,' but we appreciated the inevitability of our parents' split-up. We would've preferred somebody who was a good person."

Tina's mother also moved on, though not the way Tina would have preferred. Her mother lives with the former husband of a family friend and doesn't have any false expectations about the relationship. When Tina rethought her mother's seemingly absurd choice, it made good sense. He is the opposite of Tina's father, and her mother welcomes the routine and the comfort, and seems not to care that he's uninteresting. Tina said, "He's the master of the obvious. When he talks, you wonder why my mother doesn't throttle him. Where my father is charming, witty, and giving, her boyfriend is withholding, meticulous, and neat, but he's also very dependable—everything my father wasn't."

New Families, New Roles

As if dealing with your own parents' idiosyncrasies weren't difficult enough, enter new spouses and partners with all their relatives, children, new children, and emotional baggage. New personalities and new living arrangements make blending families a challenge. Louise's mother's

GUIDELINES FOR ACCEPTING YOUR PARENT'S NEW PARTNER

- Give the new partner a chance.
- Look for interests to share as a way to include a parent's new partner.
- Don't endanger your children's relationship with a grandparent.
- Express serious objections or concerns delicately and calmly.
- Don't be overly protective of your parent.
- Remind yourself that a parent's choice of companion is not yours to make.
- Stay in groups to help dissipate edgy or uncomfortable situations.
- If the partner is unacceptable to you, continue a separate relationship with your parent rather than sever the bond.
- Make a plan with your parent to keep in touch by scheduling get-togethers for the two of you, by calling your parent at work or at a time you know his partner will be out or away, or by e-mailing regularly.
- Maintain distance, if that's the only way to keep harmony.
- Don't put your parent in the position of having to choose between you and a new partner.
- Make concessions, if they will keep the bond to your parent strong.

third husband is what her mother has needed all her life—a caretaker—but his inflexibility and rigidity were shocking to Louise. Louise outlines some of Mario's rules:

"You can't go in the kitchen when it's not a mealtime. You can't drive the boat if you've had a beer. You have to wash your hands before dinner. He asks! I'm thirty-eight, I head one of the busiest adoption agencies in the country, and he asks me if I've washed my hands.

"I tease him a lot. I say, 'Oh, please. Give me a break.'"

Avoiding your parent's new partner may be a choice you find less nerve-racking, but it's an option that never entered Karen's mind when her father remarried. He married a compulsively organized and controlling woman, traits that greatly impinge on Karen's comfort level when she visits with her two children. Rather than being happy to be there, she feels displaced and distanced from her father. Her father's wife makes it very clear that she wants the house looking as if no one's visiting—toothbrushes must be put in a drawer, beds made, and suitcases stored out of sight. When Karen and the children arrive, she wants to know the exact day and time they plan to leave.

In order to see her father, Karen decided not to be angry about the rules. Instead she keeps an emotional distance from her father's wife, who Karen says "seems to understand instinctually and respectfully honors my desire not to be intimate with her. We have brief conversations, but the two of us would never go out to lunch together, and we steer clear of private time together. My dad senses the separation, but I know he'd rather believe we get along beautifully."

Although parents may be optimistic, adult children generally have mixed feelings about embracing and acknowledging stepbrothers and -sisters. Anne's father tells her she will have two other sisters when he and Jane are married, but Anne says, "Jane's daughters are so far removed from who I am that having a pleasant relationship with them will be difficult for me."

In contrast, Karen makes the best of sibling changes by maintaining a pleasant relationship with her stepbrothers even though they didn't live together as children. "If I'm in town, everybody gets together for the holidays," she says. "Both stepbrothers are married with children of their own, and their children and mine have cousinlike relationships. The children are all close."

Molly genuinely adores her younger half-sisters, who are much closer in age then Karen's stepbrothers are. "When my father has my kid sisters, I go wherever they are, because it's really important to me to spend time with them."

You can be pretty sure your parents want new arrangements to work out amicably as quickly as possible, expectations that may well be unfair or not possible. However, an accepting, noncommittal attitude is more constructive than patent dismissal, and down the road, you may look at the situation differently. Talia's father remarried about nine years ago, when Talia was twenty-four. Her father exerts a lot of pressure on his daughter to treat his new wife and her daughter as family members. Talia balks. "I don't consider them in the same category as my immediate family. I was already in the adult world when they married. If my father asks for something minor, I don't argue, but if I feel it's important, I tell him what's going on with me and why I'm feeling the way I am. We have reached a level of understanding of what the relationships are and what we expect. I will include his wife and her daughter in family events, but my father understands that my mother is included, too, if she's in town."

On top of asking you to include stepparents and stepfamilies in activities, your parent may offer pesky reminders of when to send birthday cards to his new partner or when you're expected at a family function. In an effort to achieve harmony, your parent may hint or request that you give up plans with your own husband or wife's family to be part of a stepparent's family gathering or celebration. When a parent is asking for or demanding your presence and you feel yourself bristling at the request, try to be pragmatic. While step- and blended families complicate adult children's lives, the new partner and his or her family can alleviate a lot of the burden, too.

There are obvious advantages in overlooking shortcomings, as Bailey, a stay-at-home mom, learned. Her mother remarried twenty years ago, when Bailey was eighteen. "I don't personally like him and don't even know his birthday. Still, I'm glad she's married and has a companion," confesses Bailey. "I think it's a bit self-serving on my part, but she has someone to do things with so she doesn't focus so much on me. He takes a bit of the pressure off me."

Whatever your age at the time of family shifts, it's wise to tell your parent how you would like his or her new partner to view and relate to you if your parent doesn't make the first move to set guidelines. Perhaps a simple request on your part, "Please ask so-and-so to stop treating me like a child." Or, "Do you think so-and-so could relax the rules when I'm around?" A passing comment about a friend's relationship with his parent's new partner may help get your point across. Be direct when asking for what you need or want from your parent or his or her partner. For example, tell your parent when needling innuendos and reminders are insulting or counterproductive.

Resentments from the past may block your acceptance of or desire to be with your parent and his or her new partner. If you are frank and honest with a parent who has angered you, the experiences lose their edge, and it becomes possible to include your parent's new partner more graciously. Gwen had a relationship with her father that was framed by the past and prevented her from spending time with him and her stepmother. Gwen's parents divorced when she was in her teens, and her father went from being the focus of her adoration to being the enemy. Rather than cutting herself off from her father or remaining angry with him, she faced the issue head-on so the relationship could progress.

"I confronted him about how he had related to me, and about all his offenses during his divorce from my mother," Gwen explains. "I screamed at him, and he listened. That was the real turning point in our relationship." Since then Gwen divides her time more or less equally between her mother and father and takes a week-long vacation alone with her stepmother every year, which was inconceivable before she spoke out. Her father's new partner became an adored addition, not a substitution for her mother.

Unraveling the Logistics

Although the choice of mates belongs solely to parents, your opinion, suggestions, feelings, and certainly actions, influence them. The more accepting you are, the easier it will be to deal with the irritants and problems inherent to blending and reblending families: Who is invited to the wedding? Who's speaking to whom? Who will be at the holiday table? With whom will you spend your or your children's birthdays this year? In spite of society's seeming

tolerance for integrating exes with new partners and assorted offspring, questions like these—and their answers—can tear at your conscience and wreak emotional
havoc within your family's' fragmented and blended
branches unless you attempt to control the situation to
some degree.

Considering how difficult it is to assemble family together and to convince feuding members to join in, you
should try to work out as much tension beforehand as
possible, and assume a peaceful, agreeable attitude for
the event itself. Louise is being married next fall and has
grave reservations about whether her father and mother
can put aside their animosity to be in the same room.
They have had no contact since their divorce. Her mother
remains very bitter over the indignities she faced at the
time of the breakup.

Louise's father is not her biological father. After marry-
ing her mother, he adopted Louise when she was five. After fourteen years of marriage he left her mother to marry
Heather, her mother's friend and neighbor. "Like my
mother, I was furious," acknowledges Louise, "but I
wanted to have a relationship with my father, and my
mother would not recognize my wishes. My mother has
remarried, too, but hasn't really gotten over the Heather
involvement. Finally I told her she needed to be an adult;
essentially I told my mother to grow up and stop acting
like a child. I don't want them to be shooting each other
dirty looks at my wedding."

Holidays, like weddings and other special occasions,
take new forms. It's nearly impossible to retain the exact
traditions you grew up with. Given new partners, children
of all ages frequently spend holidays with families they
hardly know, and trying to coordinate a satisfactory sched-

ule can create fights and jealousies. Devin's mother demanded Devin come see her on Christmas Day, but Devin refused because she wanted nothing to do with her mother's boyfriend's family, which was hosting the holiday. Like many adult children, Devin was overwhelmed by too many families—her mother's, her father's, her stepmother's, and now the mother's boyfriend's family. Devin and her mother had bitter battles until Devin expressed her true feelings

"I told my mother, 'I just want to be with you. I don't want to spend time with you and another person's family because then I'm not spending time with you.' It's been a lot easier to say, 'This is when I'm visiting for Thanksgiving or Christmas,' which is usually a day or two after the actual holiday. It's so far from the Christmas I had as a child, I don't think Christmas will feel special to me again until I have it for my own children."

You will not be able to re-create what was, but you can lessen the pain of assimilating new people into family gatherings by being flexible, by establishing new traditions, and by holding celebrations in neutral locations that are not haunted by your memories of old family traditions. Keep the focus on what is reality today.

Even with a wholehearted welcome, a new partner and his family add more factors to consider, not only around holiday celebrations but also around other important family days, vacations, and ordinary visits, times when families are normally together. Making your feelings known usually helps eliminate some of the strife. Until recently, Molly, whose parents have each had multiple marriages in the more than twenty years since their divorce from each other, was the go-between. Her mother complains that she doesn't see her daughter often enough, and her father presents the same argument. To end the friction, Molly told both parents she was tired of being in the middle, scheduling visits, passing messages, and spying. "I told them to count me out. I've forced them to tolerate each other and settle arrangements without me, and I don't feel so torn."

Seeing Things Differently

Make an effort to think of your new family constellation as extra dinners, more people to love you, your spouse, and your children (if you have them), an extended support system, and a larger portion of warm, good feelings. In short, you've gained a larger group of relatives to call your own. Just as you can change the entire feeling and perception of a picture by putting a new frame around it, you can reframe your attitude toward your parent's partner.

Daniel's feelings about his mother's boyfriend are typical of the neutral position many adult children choose to assume. "On a scale of 1 to 10 in terms of really liking someone, I rate him a 7. I was twenty-three years old when my dad died. I didn't understand grieving and working through the end of a relationship. I didn't understand the concept of closure and becoming whole again. I couldn't help my mother or guide her in that way. When the boyfriend came into the picture, I told my mother I just wanted her to be happy. I think he's a pretty insecure person; if anyone or any thought unsettles him, he gets very angry. He doesn't want to know there's trouble in paradise. He has drawbacks like we all do, but I like him, and I think he's a good-hearted person overall."

By Courtney's standards, her mother's new husband is

a nonentity, but she adopts a neutral attitude. "I definitely don't love him, but he's nice. He's kind of not there. He'll go upstairs, and I will have time alone with my mother. It's either me and my mom alone or the four of us together, my husband and him, too. I could make him an issue if I wanted to, but he's not important enough. I don't have any strong emotions toward him; the relationship is cordial, and I work hard to be friendly with him because of my mother."

In Courtney's case her stepfather pulled back and allowed Courtney and her mother room to continue their relationship as it had always been. It's more likely you will have to adapt your thinking in order to retain the closeness you had before a new person entered your parent's life.

It takes great amounts of emotional energy to fume about situations, to dislike, or to hold grudges, as well as precious time to consider all of the ramifications, the could-haves, should-haves, and would-have-beens—if only this, or if only that. There's a lot of futility in ruminating, as Peter points out: "My father's new wife is a strange bird. She's very uptight and nervous, and she makes the rest of us uptight and nervous, but we make the best of it when we're with her. I see other families who haven't had divorces, and I see what I wish we had, but I've learned that everybody's different. Yes, I think that my parents' divorce changed how we all ended up. You can't dwell on it, it's just the way it is."

For you—with a life of your own and different priorities than you had when you were younger—what's really involved? Weekend visits? Holiday meals? Occasional celebrations or vacations together? So what if your parent's choice is not ideal. Be appreciative that someone cares for and loves your parent. Being gracious takes so much less psychic time and energy, and you may indeed grow to like, even love, your parent's spouse or partner. The alterations required of you are relatively minor—slight changes or new perspectives that reflect your own maturity.

KEEPING YOUR PARENT'S NEW PARTNER IN PERSPECTIVE

- Try to figure out what triggers your negative feelings.
- Let go of dislikes and overlook small annoyances and shortcomings if your parent is happy.
- Make a mental list of the benefits for your parent, for you, and for your children.
- Don't view your parent's new partner as a parent figure; he or she is not replacing or displacing your other parent.
- Alter your thinking to focus on the good points.
- Accept that cordiality may be the best you can achieve.

SEVEN

Sibling Complications, Sibling Support

When you were growing up, warm feelings for your siblings and counting on them as best friends most likely alternated with scheming for the next time you could get them in trouble. Family strife was created by what seemed like life-altering questions: Who would ride in the front seat next to Mom or Dad? Or who would eat the last Popsicle in the freezer? Childhood quarrels, however, grew into adult issues that have powerful effects on your relationship with your parents. An adult sibling's action and parent's reaction either push the other adult children in the family away from their parents or draw them together.

Your siblings can trigger family patterns that you hoped were long buried or forgotten. A parent who worries more about one offspring than another, for example, is enough to awaken former jealousies and rekindle sibling rivalries. The resurgence of familiar competitions that once made your blood surge can dampen your parent bond.

The Family System

In adulthood, as in childhood, you assume specific roles within the family that may be a continuation of ones you held as a child or may be newly acquired. Individual slots beyond those of birth order or gender define your place in the family and what is expected. For example, a sibling may have no perceptible task because she is too busy or lives too far away to be helpful. Even the sister or brother who has little responsibility within the family has an impact on the other relationships, because you or another sibling picks up the slack, leaving room for resentment to build.

As the oldest sister, Karen's job is to keep her brother, and less so her sisters, up-to-date in their divorce-divided family. Because she does, her brother can remove himself from the family yet still feel somewhat connected, without putting much effort into the bond with either of his parents. "My brother's confident that I'll let him know what's going on because he tends not to call our mother very often," says Karen.

One sibling might be designated the consultant to whom parents turn for advice because he or she seems or is the most grounded and practical. A sister might be deemed the family medical resource because she works in a health environment. Thea, thirty-two, and her sister are two years apart, but much to Thea's dismay her mother keeps her in her younger-child mode even if the problem or issue raised is something she knows more about. If Thea wants to get a point across she must repeat it many times, but her sister needs only say it once. Their family trip to Alaska was, to Thea, just another example of her sister's opinion being more valued.

"Last year, the three of us rode horses in Alaska, looking for moose. We didn't see any, and my mother couldn't
figure out how she was going to convince her friends
Alaska had moose if she didn't have a picture. I suggested
she take a photo of a moose footprint in the mud. She told
me that was the stupidest thing she'd ever heard. An hour
later my sister presented the same solution, and my
mother thought it was a wonderful idea, immediately taking out her camera. I rolled my eyes and said nothing. I'm
getting better."

Whatever your self-defined or assumed part, it affects
all the individual connections. Ginny, thirty-four, defines
herself the "interesting daughter" and her sister, Robin, as
the "good daughter" because Robin married young and followed a traditional path. Robin, although an innocent
party, created major friction between Ginny and their parents, who had spent all their available money on Robin's
wedding. Ginny needed to borrow a few thousand dollars
to replace her car, which had been totaled in a rear-end
collision. It was the only time since she graduated from
college that she had asked her parents for money, and she
was angry and hurt when they refused.

"The good daughter was getting married, and my parents had put everything into my sister's five-hour affair.
My sister didn't want a big wedding, but it was my
mother's value, as she told me repeatedly. 'We wish you
were getting married; we would do the same for you,' my
mother said, but I know that isn't going to be possible,
since my dad has retired. To this day it *really* upsets me to
think about their refusal. When I asked about it months
later, my dad looked at me with the plainest look on his
face and said, 'You never asked before this. Your sister always asked for our help.' I remember starting to cry and

saying, 'Why should a daughter have to ask?' But you know what, for so many years without asking, how would they know and how could I expect them to help?"

Sibling Frustrations

When you take on the job of go-between, peacekeeper, or explainer, disappointments and frustrations are inevitable. One sibling is going to feel more responsible for parents than another, if only because of proximity, and one sibling is going to do more for parents. One brother may always talk a good game, but his sister always gets things done. Physical or emotional distance—or both—determines which sibling does things with and for parents. The degree to which you feel put out or resentful correlates with how you feel about the amount of responsibility. Having too much responsibility, or more than you want or are able to handle, can lead to resenting your parents.

You can reduce your burden by asking for help from your sisters and brothers, by limiting how much you do, or by accepting that this is the way things are. Nicholas has a half-brother and half-sister with whom he is close, but who ignore their mother and father—a persistent problem that Nicholas is not sure they are aware of. Nicholas takes full responsibility for their parents and never mentions his siblings' desertion. "They don't make any effort," notes Nicholas. "On holidays they don't call to make sure our parents have something to do; my brother and sister seem to think our parents are my responsibility. I don't mind, but I notice. I wouldn't have it any other way—I couldn't imagine a holiday without my parents—but they are their parents, too."

Most people are only too happy to let others take care

of what needs attention. Marcus felt his mother needed to replace her ten-year-old car and told his siblings he was thinking about buying one for her instead of telling each of them to contribute a precise amount of money. Rather than focusing on the amount of money, conversations centered on the type of car. "My one brother talked about a brand-new SUV, but I explained I could only afford a decent used car. No one offered to help, nothing. I felt as if my siblings took advantage of me. I wish I weren't the only one watching out for Mom." Being direct and asking for help from your siblings prevents a lot of agonizing. There's no guarantee his siblings would have contributed any money if Marcus had asked, but maybe they would have.

WHEN YOU WANT A SIBLING'S HELP

- Discuss your frustration with your sibling.
- Be realistic about what and how much a sibling can do.
- Offer gentle, direct reminders, not hints, of help needed. . . . If they don't work,
- Spell out what you expect and want your sibling to do,
- Or continue to assume full responsibility without complaining or feeling sorry for yourself.

Troublemakers and High-Maintenance Siblings

Unlike siblings who leave matters to another sibling or say they are too busy to be active with parents, siblings who cause family rifts add considerable stress to *your* relationship with your parents. Troublemakers can cause bitter conflict without being anywhere near the family. Christina's sister lives 300 miles from Christina and their mother, yet she insinuates herself in situations about which she knows only isolated facts. Her sister's long-distance comments create a growing wedge between Christina and her mother. "My sister manufactures ammunition out of bits of information about my fiancé that she gleans from phone calls. If my mother mentions that Jim forgets to put the toilet seat down when we're visiting, my sister pounces and turns a stupid thing like that into 'he's disrespectful'; if he forgets to run an errand for my mother, she tells my mother Jim is lazy. She has made my relationship with my mother really rough. When I had lost a lot of weight, my sister told my mother I was thin because Jim would dump me if I gained any weight. And my mother believes what my sister says! My sister met Jim once, she hardly knows him."

Troublemaker siblings who behave in insidious, deliberately hurtful ways fracture the family and often your parent connection. Wyatt's older brother refuses to accept Wyatt's homosexuality and no longer attends family functions if Wyatt brings Jack, his partner, which he usually does. When Wyatt tried to introduce Jack at a family party last summer, his brother turned and walked away. Words were exchanged, and his brother said, "Maybe my wife and I ought to leave." Wyatt's parents, who had been supportive since Wyatt divorced his wife and started seeing Jack, told his brother they thought that was a good idea. The situation tears Wyatt's parents apart because his brother has forced them to choose between their children.

Willful, acrimonious actions like those of Christina's sister and Wyatt's brother create unnecessary awkwardness and problems for parents as well as for the sibling in-volved. However, being distraught or fuming accomplishes nothing. A forceful encounter with the "troublemaker" may clarify misconceptions and minimize conflict. In both these cases, the siblings may not realize how much they are hurting their parents. Providing facts about the person or situation your sibling is spurning may explain the partic-ulars and make the problem more palatable.

Frequently a sibling who is creating havoc within the family has been acting out in detrimental ways for a long time, but sometimes an imperceptible line exists between being a troublemaker and being needy. High-maintenance siblings require—or demand—more parental time and at-tention, and in many instances financial aid goes hand in hand with their difficulties. You may have a sibling whose life is still a mess, who needs your parents' constant help with problem solving or handling his children after a di-vorce. You would think you would have adjusted to your sibling's behavior by this point in your life, but the irritat-ing behavior may needle you like a persistent low-grade fever or worse.

Forty-two-year-old corporate executive Leslie's younger brother was a problem for her growing up, but today he's thirty-eight, the father of twin boys and a girl, and how he lives his life infuriates her. According to Leslie, he acts as he did in high school, not responsible for his life. He lives at home again and expects his parents to take over for him when his children visit with him every other weekend. "My parents just let him walk all over them, the same as he did as a teenager," Leslie rages. "My parents do a lot of things with his kids during his visitation periods while he sleeps. If I say something about my brother, my mom has a fit and walks out of the house. I get angry, but I'm afraid whatever I say will cause more conflict and stress for my parents. I don't go home as much because I see my brother taking advantage of my parents."

One sibling taking advantage of parents, even when the other adult siblings are conditioned to it, disturbs family dynamics and filters back into your individual relationship with your parents, unless you are able to put aside the way you feel. To accomplish that goal, you have choices: you can either pull away as Leslie does, tolerate the situation, or accept the fact that most parents have a different set of rules and expectations for each of their offspring.

Even if you had no "sibling situations" when you were children, you now might find yourself pulled into family conflict, no matter how hard you try to avoid it. At times you may be forced by a sibling's behavior to do things you don't want to do simply to preserve your own relationship with your parents. Abigail's sister Brenda, a single mother, refuses to join the family at Abigail's in-laws for holiday dinners. Rather than balk or fight, Abigail caves in to prevent putting their father in the position of having to choose between them.

"Christmas and Thanksgiving would be so simple if it weren't for my sister," says Abigail. "The holidays get touchy, and in the end I make dinner because I think that's the best resolution, even though I don't like it. I remind my father that it's Brenda's choice; she doesn't want to come, but my father will not leave her on a holiday. In fact, he doesn't do anything without checking to see if she needs him to baby-sit. My dad is there more for my sister; but I think I've come to terms with that. Since she's single, her needs are greater than mine; I have a support system in my husband."

> ### HOW TO MANAGE PROBLEMS
> ### CREATED BY A SIBLING
>
> - Put yourself in your parents' place; they are protecting or aiding you or your siblings in ways they think best.
> - Don't discuss sibling issues or behavior with parents unless asked.
> - Accept that feelings of irritation, disgust, or displeasure with a sibling are not unusual.
> - Be aware that a sibling's life change may alter yours or your parents' lives either temporarily or permanently.
> - Separate your relationship with your parents from the one you have with your brothers and sisters as much as possible.

You Like Him Better . . . Still

Sibling rivalry is at the core of family life and almost unavoidable, even when your parents consciously work to avoid it. Rivalries may be not only about who is the best and the brightest, but also for parent attention and favor—to be the favorite child at any age. Even if parents treat each child with special care, you may mistakenly think that one sister is favored, one brother the recipient of more attention than you are.

You may sometimes wonder if you and your siblings were raised in the same household because their relationships with your parents and their memories of childhood don't often mesh with or come close to yours. Each relationship with a parent, like each child, is unique. Different types of relationships reflect individuality and temperament more than they do a parent's preference for a brother or sister. "My mother sees herself in my sister Susan," notes Courtney, "because Susan is leading my mother's life. My mother probably enjoys my middle sister Nita the best in terms of personality because she's easygoing and relaxed, low maintenance, whereas my other sister and I are high maintenance."

What you think is favoritism is more often a parent being a parent, looking out for or coming to the aid of the child who needs his help. But this kind of favoritism can be a disguise for enabling, as Grace describes. "My brother is an alcoholic and doesn't have his life together very well. He's always been my mother's favorite, and that favoritism hasn't served him well in the slightest. She excuses his behavior constantly and rewards him by telling him how funny he is when he's drunk. I suppose you could say I'm as guilty as my mother. Although I didn't encourage him in the same way, I bailed him out with money and emotional support, even moved closer to him at one point. Giving him all that attention hasn't helped one bit."

Favoritism can be vague and flighty, too. Small encounters revolving around siblings can turn a good situation better as quickly as they can turn a bad situation worse, and can change your status as the perceived favorite fairly quickly. Delia, a thirty-four-year-old woman with two children, has one sister she thinks is "from another planet. The whole family tolerates Candace, but on occasion she pushes me over the line." Candace planned their older sister's wedding, but treated Delia and her other sister as if they were the hired help, talking down to them and ordering them around. When Delia asked her to stop, Candace got huffy and stomped off; their father sided with Candace.

"I was quite upset by my father's attitude, because my father had always favored me," says Delia. "He didn't seem to care that I was in the middle of a nasty divorce and wanted support. He had been very involved with my life growing up; I did well in school, and he valued education. I was a music buff, and he loves classical music. I felt as if he had turned on me."

Delia is one of many adult children who, no matter how old they are, how successful or how mature, allows feelings of favoritism and jealousy to creep into the relationship they have with their parents. Judd, thirty-two, believes the root of the favoritism in his family stems from the facts that he is gay and his brother Paul is more like his father. "Paul has what I call the standard All-American guy thing going for him. I knew my dad loved me, but I don't think he tried very hard to appreciate or understand me.

"My sister and I joke that Paul is the favorite, and every now and then Priscilla and I refer to him as the 'favorite son.' My parents deny it, but when it comes right down to it, we all know that's the case. From my point of view, my parents do a lot more for Paul than they do for me because Paul asks them for favors, and he has a lot more opportunities to ask for favors now that he has a child and he lives close to them."

Lisa, thirty-eight, and her brother's relationships with their parents create an envy that Lisa finds unsettling. The cause is not what a sibling does or doesn't do, but barriers created by distance. Lisa lives two hundred miles from her parents, whereas her brother lives ten minutes away from them. Her parents see a lot more of her brother's son than they do of her children. Her parents play an active part in her nephew's life—her dad picks him up from day care, they have dinner with him a couple nights a week, and they see him a lot on weekends. "My mom's always talking about my nephew, what he does, how cute he is," explains Lisa. "It makes me sad that they don't have that time with my children. It's frustrating to me that my brother and his son are sharing so much more of my parents' lives than we are. It makes me feel more disconnected."

Amy also experiences the effects distance have on the relationship and perceptions of favoritism. "When you talk to my parents, you get the impression that my brother can do no wrong, and that adds tension to my relationship with my parents," complains Amy, who admits that it's embarrassing to be thirty years old and embroiled in sibling rivalries. Her brother and sister-in-law live farther away and don't see her parents nearly as often as Amy and her family do. "When my brother's around, the sun rises and sets on him. If my husband and I help out in the kitchen, we don't think twice about it; we just do what needs to get done. It's taken for granted, as it should be. But when my brother's around, and he lifts a finger, it seems like, Oh my gosh, let's celebrate.

"I think there's a certain leniency my parents afford my brother's family. If their kids are jumping on the furniture, it's okay. We have different ideas about disciplining our children. Reid and I are stricter with our children. It may be our parents following our lead, but there are differences. I also think that since they don't see my brother's family as often, they don't want any uncomfortable times when they are together.

"My parents feel very free to be as open as possible with us, even if it comes to criticism, but they don't seem to feel that way with my brother. Knowing that there's an invisible line for us makes things a bit awkward. When we are all together as a family we have a lot of fun, but I feel the tension."

What you view as favoritism or what siblings may do to influence the relationships with parents may in fact just be siblings reacting differently to parents or to their parenting styles. Seth and his brother have very individual ways of relating to their father. "My younger brother does great with my dad because he's not as headstrong as I am. He's not as passionate either. He might be annoyed with my father sometimes, but he doesn't really seem to care. Growing up, my brother would yes Dad and then do his own thing. My tack is to argue it out. I confront things; my brother says whatever and goes about his own way."

Understanding Favoritism

- Is it favoritism, or is your parent helping a sibling in different ways because each of you has different needs?
- Recognize that each sibling is an individual who will be treated differently by different people, including your parents.
- Look for the light or humorous side of favoritism.
- Accept your role in the family system; if you're unhappy with it, redefine it by changing how you react or behave.

Sibling Assistance

Rather than being jealous or frustrated by a sibling, take advantage of the qualities that make your sibling different from you to enrich the relationship you all have with your parents. Adult children acting in tandem and being supportive in areas that pertain to parents can improve another sibling's parent relationship as well as make specific situations more pleasant. Siblings can be there when you can't, break troublesome news to your parents to soften the blow, or help you convince a parent when change is needed. Siblings can take the focus or onus off you or be your advocates with parents. In sum, when they're in your camp, siblings can make your relationship with your parents easier or better than it already is.

Inge and her sister have distinctive roles in their relationship with their parents. Inge satisfies concrete, practical needs, while her sister meets their parents' emotional needs. As a joint effort, their individual contributions complement each other and serve to enhance each daughter's relationship with her parents. Inge's sister takes the burden off Inge, who consequently doesn't feel a day-to-day obligation. "My sister has kids, and my mom is crazy about them. My sister probably talks to my mother three times a day and sees her three times a week; she's more attached emotionally and by geography than I am. I make the quick five-second call and can help them sort out financial matters. If I decide to go away for Thanksgiving, I don't have to feel guilty because I know my sister will be with them. It's a huge relief not to have to worry about them on a daily basis."

Siblings who pull together can relieve a parent of having too much responsibility for a sibling in need or distress. When Vanessa's brother-in-law died, leaving her sister with two small children, Vanessa, her brother, and her other sister pitched in by rotating who stayed with her and helped her with the children. They helped her through her grief and later baby-sat so she could return to

---

MAXIMIZING SIBLING SUPPORT

- Don't operate in a vacuum.
- Predetermine who will do what with and for parents.
- Devise compromises all siblings can live with.
- Work together to clarify and solve parent and/or sibling problems.
- Take time when siblings are together to discuss issues that involve all of you.
- Reduce sibling competitiveness by joining forces in planning celebrations, scheduling holiday events, or buying gifts for parents.

---

school. Not only were they helping their sister, they helped their mother, who would have shouldered the entire load.

A sibling can also be influential in preserving your relationship with parents whose shortcomings or misunderstandings don't allow them to act like the parents you wish you had. When one of Richard's sisters became pregnant and decided to have an abortion, she could not turn to her mother for support; she called Richard. "I took the logical approach," he says. "I found my sister a clinic, and got an appointment for the abortion. One of my other sisters told my mother about it several months later. Hearing the news after the fact cushioned the blow and made it easier for my mother to absorb and accept."

You may be called on to intervene for your brother or sister because you are less emotionally involved or can more easily pave the way in a given situation. Or you may see how hurt one of your siblings is by your parents' ac-

tions or reactions, but you can approach the problem—
and your parents—from a different perspective and present a different outlook. By coming to your sibling's
defense, you may be able to stop bad feelings from esca-
lating or prevent a break in your sibling's relationships
with your parents.

EIGHT

Money Matters

Money has a striking impact on any personal relationship, including the one between you and your parents. There may be generational differences in philosophies about money as well as individual differences. Depending on how finances are managed between you and your parents, money matters either burden your relationship or free it. The way people choose to handle money can erect walls or open up a new sense of sharing and mutuality.

Although in some parent-adult child relationships money is inconsequential and rarely mentioned, in others—the majority—some aspect of money is of deep concern. For instance, you may cringe at the way your thrifty parents save money, while your parents may be nervous about your spending habits. You may feel money is a private issue, but your parents pry into your money affairs, or you could feel the opposite, disappointed by their lack of interest. Even if you share similar values with your parents, chances are that money disparities arise from time to time, requiring you to examine your attitudes and possibly rethink your approach to financial affairs involving your parents.

Not adopting or not being able to live up to a parent's values regarding money strains the relationship when it produces a nagging feeling of not being "good enough" or not achieving what a parent wanted. Karen and her father have a different sense of money and its importance. Karen, a nurse, and her husband, a college admissions officer, don't have the same luxuries her father subscribes to, neither do they particularly want them. She knows how important these extras are to him, probably because he grew up with nothing and made a success of himself. Although her father doesn't say anything, she senses his disappointment that she and her husband don't meet his criterion for financial success. Like other adult children, she would like to please her father, but she has accepted the fact that his way of life is unlikely for her and her husband. She does not allow her feelings related to money to define her relationship with her father; instead, she defines it by the closeness and warmth they share.

The difference between Karen's father and Courtney's mother is that in addition to wanting the luxury and prestige money confers for her daughter, Courtney's mother sees money as the critical factor in a woman's relation to her partner. While Courtney, who has been married for a year, has kept her job as an administrative assistant for a professional sports team, her sister relies on her husband for financial support. "My sister's husband earns a lot of money in the insurance business, and my mother admires that. When my sister and her husband had no money, my mom felt badly for them and complained about her husband's inability to support my sister. Now that my brother-in-law has done well, my mother is a very happy person. She thinks not working defines a woman. I try to tell her I choose to work, just as I chose not to change my name when I got married, but she doesn't get it. When we talk about the future, she says, 'Hopefully you won't have to work.' I say, 'Hopefully I'll have the choice.'"

A parent's concern about your finances may feel like disappointment to you. Or you may see it as love, welcomed assistance, insinuation, or control. When your interpretation is negative, money can create friction and become a constant barb that fractures the bond you have.

Every relationship has downfalls. For Kim, a married, thirty-year-old occupational therapist with one toddler, it's money, and her father's intrusion is not dissimilar from what she experienced with him as a child. Money is the only issue she ever has with her father. His relentless probing feels no different than it did when Kim was spending her allowance on comic books, candy bars, and music. "I'm a grown woman, and he's still asking questions that make me squirm. Money issues are always tense, and I try to change the conversation because I don't want to get yelled at—as if I were a kid doing the wrong thing!" Her husband thinks Kim's father is interested, but to her it feels like harassment. Her husband thinks her father's questions send a message of love, because his parents never ask him such things.

When parents take so-called interest beyond questions, the invasion can feel like an attack on your very being. Jessica, thirty-four, used part of the small sum she inherited from her grandmother to pay her family's insurance and planned to use the balance to attend a dear friend's wedding. Her father felt she should have saved the money, forcing Jessica to defend her decision. "What hurts," says Jessica, "is that my parents don't give me any credit. My parents are always looking over our shoulders to see what's going on with money. They have to know how we're going to pay for this or that and where the money is coming from. Financial stress is very hard, and my parents don't make it any easier."

Receiving Money from Your Parents

As difficult as it is to need or ask for financial help or to have your parents interfering, it can be just as problematic to accept their money. Depending on how your parents offer money, you may feel irritated and demeaned or boxed in and controlled. The word *control* crops up frequently in conversations about money and parents. Unusual or unavoidable conditions as well as the high cost of living today may put you in the position of having to ask for or take money from your parents.

Thirty-year-old Jana has a six-week-old baby whose father she doesn't want in her life. She goes to school and works part-time. Her parents are providing a roof over her head, meals, and help with the baby. Jana understands that "those things come at a cost: if my father has something to say, I have to listen to him. It's easy to control someone when you're paying her bills. He's generous and wants to be involved in the baby's life, but when it's controlling—and my father is that—and emotional, it's a real thorn. For now I'm stuck."

Jana's situation is temporary, caused by extenuating circumstances. But, when you have been receiving money for many years, it can hold you hostage. And when you get accustomed to the money, it's difficult to break the habit.

Morgan, thirty-seven, felt not only controlled by her parents' money but also tied to them by it. Her parents gave her everything she wanted, but she felt they were giving her things and money instead of parental interest or care. She relied on her parents to cover her bills while she had a string of low-paying jobs, followed by years of special training and education to become an interpreter at the United Nations. Morgan admits that she really never learned about money because she wasn't earning it. "I was afraid to make the break from my parents' money. I felt if I give up the money, I give up the relationship. I believe they felt the same way."

You can also find yourself a prisoner of your parents, if money is so liberally given that you never learn to take care of yourself. Like Morgan, Flora, who will turn forty in a few months, is aware of the predicament she's in. "My parents raised me as a rich princess," concedes Flora. "Since my divorce, I can't afford the lifestyle I'm accustomed to, and my parents dangle money in front of me like a carrot." If Flora wants to buy a chair for her house or send one of her children on an expensive trip, she has to get her parents' permission because she can't do it without their money. She's spoiled, no question, and doesn't know how to live modestly, yet is quick to admit that she can't seem to give up what she's used to doing and having.

Money as a means of control usually brings several highly charged emotions into play simultaneously. For instance, your parents may give you money not only to express their love but also to get you to do what they wish or what they think is best for you. In Joyce's case, her father had applied money pressure to bribe her since she was a teenager. Joyce had a weight problem almost all of her life, and her father would offer her a reward if she would lose twenty pounds. "I'm a mother now, with two children, and he's still at it. He wrote me a really beautiful letter telling me how he had struggled with weight at times in his life, how he believes I'm an amazing mother, raising amazing kids, and that I should lose weight so I'll be alive to enjoy my children. He offers to pay for any personal trainer or any weight-loss program I choose, and to buy me a new wardrobe when I lose the weight. Tempting? Not in the least. Everyone knows losing weight is something a person has to be motivated to do on her own."

MONEY THAT OBLIGATES YOU

Your parents offer money to encourage you to stop smoking, to stop dating someone they don't care for, to finish college, or to visit more, among many other things. Sometimes parents' motives are pure, and other times the offer is designed to deliver the result parents seek. Even when your parents provide money, in large or small amounts, with no strings attached, you may assume a degree of indebtedness unless your connection has been severely damaged. More often than not, accepting money from your parents—whether it is for the down payment on a house or to help with grandchildren's tuitions or camp fees—may make you feel as if you have to reciprocate in some way.

At forty-six, Amos went through a midlife crisis that culminated in satisfying a two-decade desire to own a Mercedes that he could ill afford. He decided he had waited long enough and asked his father for help. When Amos and his wife want to take a vacation and don't have the money, his father sends a check with a note saying something like, "See the world, don't stay home." Amos doesn't think the checks are a big deal in terms of trying to buy him, but he does feel an obligation to call and visit his father more often than he might do otherwise.

Amos's father is not as successful in "buying" his daughter's time. Amos's sister accepts money from their father for just about everything, but still ignores him. Their father doesn't see Beth or his grandchildren, but he keeps sending her money, hoping it will change the dynamic. Beth can't be moved. They are both ornery and had an extremely adversarial relationship the whole time Beth was growing up. She blames his verbal abusiveness and manipulation for the problems she has today.

Kenneth felt a pervasive dread about his mother, knowing her demanding nature and the implications of being indebted to her. "As soon as I finished my education," he says, "my prime motivation in life was to make sure I made my own money so I didn't have to be controlled by hers. My sister hasn't been able to free herself; she isn't rolling in dough, and my mother helps her out regularly. Because of the money, my sister has a guilt-ridden orientation toward my mother. She feels she has to include her for holidays, then I get to listen to how awful Mother behaved."

PARENTAL INVOLVEMENT IN YOUR FINANCIAL AFFAIRS

Financial advice, just like money itself, can be a control device. Depending on how your parents handle this emotionally laden issue, getting their input can be beneficial. Some people are comfortable using their parents as financial advisers and money managers, relying completely on their parents' experience and expertise. But most adults, whether or not they have a solid grasp of financial matters, don't want a parent insinuating him or herself in their financial life. Be specific about the type of money-related help you want from your parents; they can help you without getting into every nook and cranny of your financial information. You might ask a parent what she thinks is the best way to pay off your credit card debt at a low rate. You might approach a parent and say, I have x amount of dollars to invest; where do you think I should put it? Or ask where they have invested lately. What stocks or bonds do they think are a wise investment right now? Keep any arrangements simple so there's little room for misunderstanding.

Advice is one thing; business transactions with the investment of real dollars are another. You may come out of financial dealings with parents unscathed, but if there are lingering entanglements with a controlling parent, you may be facing tough times. Deliberate displays of control have the potential to destroy your relationship. When Sharon was thirty-one, she bought a condominium at the top of the market with her parents so she would have a place to live and they would have a good investment. Her father provided part of the down payment and added his name to the title. Ten years later everything pointed to getting rid of the apartment—the neighborhood was in decline, more desirable buildings were going up in better areas, and the apartment needed a fortune in repairs—but her father was distraught about the lost value and refused to sell. Sharon and her father were locked in disagreement.

Her father was so angry he would not talk to Sharon. Offering to give him the money—all he had put in—made him crazier and more irrational. Sharon details her ordeal. "He screamed at the lawyer. Nothing could calm him because he had lost control over the apartment. He has issues about control anyway, and this put him over the edge.

I was firm, we had a buyer, and we were selling. He was driving me away. Through my mother, I made the point that he was losing a daughter over twenty thousand dollars. Was it worth it? was the question I posed." Sharon's question, a last attempt to harness his irrationality, worked, but it will be the last time she commingles monies with her father.

Claiming Rights to Your Parents' Money

You may feel that your parents should give you money because you are in dire financial trouble, or because it is just a nice thing to do for a child. Or you may feel you're entitled to your parents' monetary support because you've been an excellent son or daughter or because you have put up with the endless trials of your difficult parent.

Nancy, a fifty-year-old, divorced, out-of-work newspaper reporter, finds herself enraged when her eighty-two-year-old father refuses to give her money. She experiences a combination of resentment of and disappointment in her father and lashes out in frustration. "He's a tightwad, always has been. He knows I'm in financial straits and have to mortgage my house to keep going, but he's told me, 'I'm not giving you any money.' I sometimes wonder if he cares if I wind up on the street."

You, too, may be quick to criticize your parents or in-laws, but the fact is that as parents age, being financially self-sufficient becomes their top priority, and for some a matter of pride. Giving you money depletes your parents' bank accounts and makes them fearful that they won't be able to pay for their own needs later in life. Few parents want to rely on their adult children for financial support. Without question parents of adult children, especially older parents, become anxious about outliving their money, and that's something to consider when judging your parent's lack of generosity.

Although little excuses the parent who is plain tight-fisted, looking elsewhere in the relationship helps keep friction to a minimum. Amanda wrestles with her father's pecuniary ways and concludes, "He's a very cheap person and always has been. If he gives me stamps, he asks me to repay him, and I do. It's easier than getting into it. When I got married, my dad didn't want to pay for the wedding because he felt I was old enough to be able to pay for it myself. I was quite angry for a while, but I resolved it by telling myself he's the parent I'm closest with, and he was always there for me as a kid. Anything he does is not as bad as my mother, who walked out on us. You pick your battles."

Misreading your parents' feelings about money can jeopardize your relationship. Insight into their parenting ideals sheds considerable light. The way parents handle money is often predicated on parenting beliefs that may seem unjust to you when they give to a sibling and not to you. Your sister or brother, however, may not earn as much or handle money as wisely as you do. Devin's parents made a habit out of supporting her brother long after he finished college. When she needed to borrow money, they said no. She felt terribly rejected, and told her father so. "My father showed no remorse at the inequity. He told me he and my stepmother give me emotional support, which is true, and they give my brother money. When I calmed down, I realized my brother and I live different lives; it wasn't worth getting that upset over."

You may have parents who put such a premium on raising independent, financially aware children that you are unwilling to engage in money discussions with them. Richard's parents had such strong feelings about what they wanted and expected from their children, that he said, "I would do anything in the world to avoid asking my parents for money, and every one of my brothers and sisters would do the same. We've gotten ourselves into predicaments just like anybody does; we loan each other money, but not one of us would go to our parents. To my parents, being self-supportive was paramount. You didn't want to go to Mom or Dad for money because you failed them if you had to do that. I wouldn't put myself through the embarrassment."

When your marriage or your parent's remarriage exposes you to other parental values, you may encounter stark differences in attitudes toward money to which you will have to adjust. Wendy, forty, sees a huge distinction between her parents and her in-laws: "With my parents, their children and grandchildren are a priority. If we need a refrigerator or washing machine or the children want piano lessons, my parents are right there with the checkbook. My father-in-law's approach to money is that not having money toughens you up. He is adamant that his children will not have any of his money until he's dead."

Few problems focus attention on money or bring out feelings of entitlement and injustice more than a parent's death. When coupled with the deep loss, the possibilities for destroying the relationship with your living parent loom large. "One of my parents' neighbors invited my father to dinner when she came back to our house not hours after putting my mother in the ground," John Jr. reports.

"It was so indecent, I wanted to throw her out. She was the widow stalking, preying on my dad who had just buried his wife."

John's father's perspective was completely different; he saw Jeanette as a kind woman who had lost her husband several years earlier and was simply being neighborly. She was as surprised as John Sr., sixty-two, and his children when, over the next few months, they found themselves enjoying one another's company and support. They fell in love and decided to get married eight months later. John Jr., along with his younger brother and sister, stopped speaking to their father. The children took the swiftness of the match as an affront to their mother's memory, and their feelings intensified, rather than dissipated, over time. The separation so upset John Sr. that he consulted a therapist to find out how to help his children understand that he loves Jeanette and that they each fill what would have been a lonely void left by the deaths of their respective spouses.

Although John Sr. did not resolve the conflict with his children in therapy, he came away with a profound realization. "I have a right to a full life and to share it with someone I love. That love came faster than my children thought was respectful, but I'm not giving up the chance, not in my sixties, to be with someone I care about. It's truly their loss. I hope they'll come around, but they may not. And that's too bad for all of us."

The real anger often revolves around money—a fear that the new spouse will inherit their parent's estate. Rather than let the relationship with a parent dangle on a no-contact, unpleasant plateau, ask your parent outright what the arrangements are. You may be pleasantly surprised to discover that your parent has addressed finances in a manner that protects you and your siblings.

When Parents' Generosity Makes You Uncomfortable

Most parents are proud when they achieve a financial level that permits them to give money freely to their adult children. Your parents may feel responsible for helping you, whether or not you need the money. They may also see their generosity as compensation for the things they couldn't afford when you were growing up or for time they didn't spend with you. Some parents experience pure delight at being able to give, to send a check with no restrictions on its use, to set up savings accounts for their grandchildren, or to provide money for house repairs.

If you need money, let's say to help you meet mortgage payments temporarily, having family backing during hard times is very reassuring and in some situations can save you from being forced to make traumatic and major life changes. Yet help in any form, especially if it seems excessive, can lead to emotional conflict between spouses. Samantha's parents are very generous and supportive, but every time they want to do something to help, Samantha goes through a trying period with her husband. "My husband has a lot of baggage about how I supported our family for six years while he finished graduate school, and then when he starts being the primary breadwinner, when he has a paycheck that will put us on the better side of town, he doesn't want their money anymore."

Here are logical arguments Samantha presented to

help her husband over the "acceptance hump." They can easily be modified to meet your individual circumstances.

- It's not about needing things, it's about luxuries my parents can afford.
- They have the money, and if they want to spend it, think of it as them spending it on their grandchildren, not on us. Our kids are as much their grandchildren as they are our kids.
- They want their grandchildren to have more fun, to be in a safer environment—think of it that way.
- We could get by without their help; we could live in a smaller house, we don't have to live in this neighborhood. The children could go to a different day camp, but think about it, they're going to *love* this day camp.
- My parents want to help us; they can afford to do it; they're not putting themselves out in any way. This amount of money is a much larger percent of our bank account than theirs.
- They don't want us to feel we have to scrimp and save in any way to pay them back soon.
- The money means a lot to us, but it doesn't mean that much to them.
- Their ability to help us is gratifying to them; it's pay-off to me from my dad for being a workaholic for thirty-something years and not being around when I was a teenager.
- Now he is able to support us and be the grandfather in a way he couldn't be a father.

Samantha's arguments are convincing, but emotions and the natural inclination to compare families remain strong; as a result, convincing your spouse or partner to be gracious is usually more complicated. For your partner, the issue can be loaded with elements of not feeling good about himself and/or having parents who can't be or don't want to be as helpful

Parents who don't have the financial resources to help their children also may feel badly that your in-laws give you what they cannot. Abigail is house-poor, like many other young adults with young children, and her father worries about her family's finances but is unable to help, although he would like to. Her husband's parents can do more monetarily. "My dad would if he could," Abigail defends her father. "I remind him of the helpful things he does that money doesn't buy. He baby-sits for me, and if other children are here, he plays with all of them. He has a relationship with his grandchildren that's solid and comfortable, something my husband's parents don't have."

Reassuring your parent of her importance in your life and your appreciation for the things she does with and for you and your children helps immeasurably in lessening a feeling of financial inadequacy. Karen's parents divorced when she was fifteen. Her father is in an excellent financial position, but her mother is not. "I know she feels down because she would love to take us all to Disney World or on a ski vacation. She doesn't have the money to take trips, but we couldn't care less, because that's not what we expect from her. I love the time she spends with my sons, and she knows it."

At times it's difficult to receive monetary gifts from parents, whatever the circumstances, but before you put the brakes on your parents or in-laws, consider how they might be feeling. Giving to you may be one of your parents' greatest joys in life, a fact to consider when you're conflicted about accepting their generosity.

COPING WITH AND UNDERSTANDING PARENTS' GENEROSITY

- When you feel you cannot refuse a monetary gift, accept it warmly; spend it on your children or donate it to a charity.
- Show appreciation when parents help you meet a financial crisis or attain your goals.
- Respect, or at least acknowledge, your partner's feelings about incoming or outgoing monies that involve parents.
- Some parents want to spend their money while they are alive; feel fortunate to be the recipient.
- If parents' generosity causes conflict with a spouse, let your parents know.
- Think about the joy your parent may be experiencing by helping you financially.
- Understand that parents who give their adult children money may still worry and feel protective of you.
- Don't compare parents and in-laws in the financial arena.
- For parents who can't help out financially, underscore other positive things they do for you and your family.

Parents Needing Financial Help from You

You may be in good financial position to help your parents if they hit a financial snag, or to give them a luxury they can't afford. When you are on the giving end, you need to pay close attention to how your generosity may affect your relationship with your parents. As in all money relations with parents, you are in sensitive territory. Parents who have poor money management skills or are financially irresponsible make the decision to help especially difficult. Thirty-five-year-old Mya has been frustrated by her mother's imprudent money management for many years and lends her mother money when she sees she's struggling. Her mother is a health care manager in a large hospital and makes a decent salary, which should be enough for her rent, car payments, and living expenses, but she doesn't know how to budget and/or spend appropriately. "I wind up filling in with what she's missing," says Mya, "and it doesn't make me happy."

Her parent's poor money management forced Stephanie, who earns more than triple her father's highest salary, to partially subsidize their move to a smaller home in the same area, decorating, and most recently the purchase of a much-needed computer to help her father put together a résumé and find a new job. Initially Stephanie worried that her support might feel emasculating to her father, but he said he was proud that his daughter had done so well. After eight years of providing money, Stephanie reveals her exasperation. "My mom can't decide which computer to buy, and for weeks she goes back and forth between brands. One day she says, 'Okay, I think we're going to go for the Dell, what do you think?' I say, 'If it were up to me I'd buy any brand, just buy it. Dad needs a job.' She says, 'Oh, I wish we were getting you the computer instead of your buying us one.' I hadn't thought about it from her point of view before; I was too busy being angry about her procrastination. Unlike my father, my mother is depressed when she needs financial help from her children."

As despondent as Stephanie's mother is about receiving help from her daughter, there are parents who take their adult children's assistance for granted and take advantage no matter how extensive the help is. Lila and her husband, Bill, both in their mid-forties, have been supporting Lila's parents for years. Because of bad choices and heavy spending during their working years, her parents had little money for retirement. Lila and Bill bought them a condominium in Arizona and pay the monthly maintenance and mortgage. When her parents needed a new car, Lila agreed to a lease up to $200 per month. "Instead of being thankful, my dad called and told me about a car he wanted to lease for $250 a month," explains Lila. "I feel guilty saying $200 a month for a car is enough, but their payments on top of ours put a lot of pressure on us.

"My mother whines that the trips they take aren't as exclusive as those their friends take. Their sense of entitlement is beyond me. We're supporting them. My job is fairly secure, but my husband works in the fragile technology industry. He's been a good sport about sharing my parents' expenses, but we both are having difficulty with their implication that I owe them. At some point, Bill is going to stop being a nice guy, or if he loses his job, we're not going to be able to keep my parents in the style they've become accustomed to."

It's unlikely that you will be able to convince your parents to drastically alter their spending habits or to live more modestly. Harder still is to pull out once you're immersed in a lifesaving or lifestyle-enhancing mode. Therefore, it's wise to assess your parent's total financial picture and history with money before committing to advancing money for her latest financial predicament. Sarah thought paying off her mother-in-law's credit card debt would make a nice birthday gift, but her husband, Drew, knew his mother's failings with money. "We're not loaded, but we're happy to give back," Sarah says. Drew was firm; he refused to pay her credit card bill. Initially Sarah argued with him until he explained how his mother spends a lot of money on her dogs—a dozen of them, strays she finds on the street. She paid thousands for a kidney transplant for one of them. Drew thinks the transplant was ridiculous. "If it's not her animals, it will be something else, is Drew's point, and he's probably right," Sarah grants.

If you limit help to what you can easily afford, you can avoid getting into messy situations with your parents as well as putting undue financial pressure on yourself. Lynn, a thirty-one-year-old psychology student, and her husband are newlyweds with no financial reserves. They can't help her widowed mother, who is financially okay right now but could use help, so Lynn and her husband do small things. When they visit, they pick up groceries or wine or something her mother needs for the house—a new garden hose or kitchen trash can. "My mother appreciates that we think about her. If I could change anything, I'd change my financial status so I could help her more. She knows we're going to take care of her when, as she says, 'the well runs dry.'"

Unlike Lynn and her husband, Inge and Keith are older, established, with considerable discretionary income. The difference in Inge and her parents' income opened the door for Inge to be supportive sooner, rather than later in her parents' lives. Inge shares her good fortune by offering her parents experiences they would not be able to afford on their modest income.

Taking your parents on extended vacations, buying them airline tickets so they can be part of family celebrations, or treating them to dinner and the theater are wonderful gifts, but you should be mindful of how your parents might feel. Some parents feel guilty if they can't reciprocate. When situations become too one-sided, your parents may feel inadequate.

"We can get away with the theater thing about ten times in a row and then my mother, out of embarrassment or pride or both, announces that we can buy the tickets but they are buying dinner, or they will not come and she means it." Inge nods for emphasis. "They want a sense that they are doing something for us, too." To retain a semblance of balance, Inge's mother prepares and stocks their freezer with foods she knows they like, and her father acts as handyman/electrician, handling jobs Keith doesn't know how to do.

Even when you are fully aware of how parents feel about money matters, lending or giving money can be confounding whatever end of the money machine you are on. There's a lesson in Stephanie's story, be you the adult child receiving money from your parent or the adult child handing it out. "One of the joys I have when I spend time with my parents is taking them out for decadent things I know they wouldn't ordinarily do or would feel stressed doing. But they take the fun away because I know they're adding up all the extras, and that irritates me.

"I like bags, expensive bags, something my mother would never spend money on. She's got fine taste, she's quite an elegant lady, and I wanted to get her something special. As soon as she opened the box, her eyes lit up, she loved the bag. Two seconds later she said, 'You shouldn't be spending your money on it.' I said, 'It's my money; I chose to do this.'"

DOLLAR SENSE—TIPS FOR HANDLING MONEY MATTERS

- Don't talk to everybody else; speak truthfully and directly to your parent if you have a problem with your parent's money management or decisions.
- Take some time to examine and possibly alter your perspective before overreacting.
- Try to find a mutually agreeable course of action for everyone involved.
- Allow for differing money philosophies.
- Deciding not to help your parents is a perfectly acceptable decision.
- Separate money issues from other aspects of your relationship.
- Don't let money dictate the character of your relationship.

NINE

Career Directions
and Decisions

You probably have basked in your parents' elation when you succeeded beyond their expectations, and have been devastated by their disappointment when your career stalled or hit a downward trajectory. Being overlooked for a promotion or raise or not being able to find a job is bad enough without having to deal with your parents' sadness. At any age, you are your parents' child, and they feel your pain, disenchantment, or frustration in much the same way they did when you weren't invited to a friend's fifth birthday party, when you failed a test, or when you didn't make the team.

Their protective instincts and hopes for you to be recognized don't disappear because you're thirty or fifty years old—which explains why many parents are quick to give advice, and lots of it. Whether or not you follow your parents' prescribed route, you could have a parent who offers nonstop job pointers, even in a field he or she knows nothing about.

Your competency in your chosen field may elude your parents entirely because you work in an area unknown to them. As jobs become more specialized and complex, parents require explanations about new industries and opportunities and details about children's accomplishments in what to them is largely an informational black hole.

You may have a parent who wanted you to be an astronaut, a Pulitzer Prize–winning author, an architect who designs skyscrapers, or a member of the police force, as he and his father had been. Parental ambitions and family traditions die hard among career choices. Making parents understand your choice is complicated if a parent was set on your entering a particular occupation or the family business.

Parental advice often appears rather transparent: a parent who wants his child to follow in his footsteps; a parent who doesn't; a parent who seeks wish fulfillment for his or her own missed opportunity; a parent who believes a sizable income is the only measure of success. Where you are now in your career need not continue to contribute to difficult times with parents or damage the ongoing relationship. It's not a question of deciding who is or was right or wrong or if you should or should not bend to your parents' wishes. Rather, make an effort to focus on the good aspects of your parents' input, the actions that helped them succeed and be happy. By first understanding your parents' expectations, you can better understand their pressures, views, and concerns. To progress toward a closer, more positive relationship, acceptance and understanding of your parents' position is paramount. When they see you happy and successful, their attitude may change.

Great Expectations

Many parents measure their parenting success by how well their children fare professionally. While growing up, you were influenced and pressured not only by your parents' hopes and dreams for your choice of life work but also by your parents' fields of interest, jobs, or the kind of people your parents were or had hoped to be. "My mother wanted me to go into politics, but then she's an extreme activist," chortles Debra, forty-one, who is the patient relations coordinator for a large private hospital. She describes her father as "a philanthropist of the soul who enjoys doing things for people," who volunteers for community service projects, works with children, and cleans up trash from streets every day. In school their dual influence kicked in, and it seemed quite natural for Debra to go into an advocacy field.

Parental influence can push you away from your parents' preferences just as readily as it sends you headlong in their desired direction. Although parents have a reason for wanting you to pursue a particular course, their rationales and how they direct their children have unique flavors. Isabelle's father, a high school principal, predetermined educational paths for his daughters—one was to be a veterinarian, the other a doctor (his own dream). When her sister decided to become a computer engineer, their father was beside himself. Unlike her sister, Isabelle has pretty much followed his ordained course. "I don't think I've ever seen anybody so happy in my entire life as my father on the day I graduated from medical school," Isabelle recalls. "He smiled at me and said, 'You've made me the happiest father who's ever been alive, and now I can die with a smile on my face.' Is he proud? Definitely, I've no doubt. I think he looks at me and sees everything he feels he never fulfilled in his own life."

For some parents, their prodding has a strong financial component. About the time Doug, thirty-two, and his sister, Rachael, thirty, were thinking about college and careers, managed care was instituted, and their parents, both doctors, were experiencing marked income declines. Their parents began an intense campaign to steer them away from medicine. Over dinner they reminded their children how stressful their lives were; how difficult it was to raise a family when one or both were rushing out to handle an emergency; how managed care had drastically reduced their earning power, and it would get worse. Rachael was relieved because she never wanted to be a doctor; for Doug, the decision was more difficult, because he had gone on rounds with their father every Saturday morning for as long as he could remember, and until halfway through high school had planned to be a pediatrician. Neither child became a physician; Doug has a promising career in the recording industry with potential to earn big money, and Rachael is thrilled with her job as a social worker.

When your parents' wishes are so strong and voiced repeatedly, you may, like Doug, give up your own dreams to satisfy your parents, though you may also wind up feeling conflicted. Ron gave into his father's pressure and is a counselor for abused teens who live in state residences, a step far away from his desire to become a painter. Nevertheless, Ron retains that dream for himself. "My father is very bullheaded," says Ron, thirty-six. "Being an artist didn't seem smart or logical to my father." Ron's father is a realist and wanted him to be able to support himself. The steady income is essential now that Ron is married, but he would never admit it to his father. Ron likes to think he would have been happy painting and being poor. He paints on the weekends and puts his watercolors in small local shows. "My father still tells me pursuing art is foolish, but at this point in my life I ignore him."

Your parents can send career signals without saying a word. Lisa's father always told his children that anything was possible, that they could do whatever they wanted in terms of job choice, but Lisa, thirty-eight, always felt her father, a chiropractor, was disappointed with his career choice. "He's quite artistic and handy and would have been happier in a field that utilized those talents. I design restaurant space, so in a strange way I got his signal, and I'm doing what he wanted to do."

You may follow your parent's overt or covert lead even if you rebuffed his career direction and pressure. Steve, a forty-five-year-old financial consultant, assesses where he finds himself today. "For all my talk about not doing what my father wanted, I do the exact same thing he did and followed almost the exact same course. I do financial consulting; he did the same; I started in bonds; he started in bonds; I switched, just as he had in his career, to managing funds."

Going into the Family Business

If your parents have a successful, going enterprise, they usually want to insure it by having you or a sibling join the organization. Your parents will employ either a gentle nudge or a hard push to have their dream fulfilled. Some parents feel that their children shouldn't have to start over; rather, they should step in and take over the family business—and a few adult children need no encouragement, it's what they've always wanted. On the face of it, joining your parent's company seems logical, inviting, and a sure bet until you consider the complications: other relatives in the business, personality differences, divergent work styles, or ethical disparities. Some problems can be ironed out, while others, for the sake of salvaging your parent-child bond, preclude merging family members in the same office.

Peter's father had hoped all his children would join his investment business, but only Peter was willing to try. Peter and his father worked together for six years, and although they sometimes had differences, they didn't really battle. But with Peter's cousins in the business, too, family issues were always popping up, and Peter left to start his own investment firm, a mutual decision with no hard feelings. He works in an area that doesn't compete with his family's company.

When you contemplate joining your parents' business, you'll go through a range of emotions, and once you're employed, there will be considerable ups and downs before arrangements work out. After college Seth spent a year in England working for a joint venture company, then returned to the States. Considering marriage and thinking working with his father and brother would be lucrative, he joined the family's furniture manufacturing company for an unhappy three years. Seth hated being in his father's shadow, didn't feel good about being the boss's son, and thought he wasn't accomplishing anything on his own.

Seth stepped away for several years, worked for another company, and returned, yielding to excessive pressure from his father. This time Seth had fresh ideas and a different attitude; he was more expressive of his needs and more understanding of his father's personality and office persona. "We've entered a period of mutual respect," Seth reports. "I confront my father, who hates confrontation on any level, but the conflict diffuses and we're back to normal. I work a lot harder than my brother, and I asked for more money. My father blew up but gave me a raise a few days later. It took a while to resolve our differences, but I actually enjoy the fun of building personal relationships in sales and the creativity of marketing. We all do different things, so he and my brother don't get into my territory, and I don't get into theirs. Having been away, I recognized that I had a lot to offer. Once we worked out the problems, I was glad I did."

The clashing of wills can be intense when your parents want to pass on a thriving business, and you show no interest. Eric grew up being primed for just that and never had an option to do anything else. The pressure to achieve, to go to the right school, to be the best, and to be productive was always present for Eric. His father had visions of adding another Chadwick to Chadwick, Inc., his father's fashion design group; when Eric was in college his father often mentioned making it Chadwick and Chadwick or Chadwick and Son. Eric describes his father as domineering, opinionated, and brilliant. "You could say, formidable," summarizes Eric, who dislikes both fashion and the retail business. "I love animals and wanted to be a vet. What I wanted didn't mesh with my father's desire. It was a lot of years of bucking his iron nature. We weren't meant to be in business together; that was some wild fantasy of his."

Beyond your dislike of or lack of suitability for the business your parents own, opposing values and ethics can make joining forces with your parents not worth the upset or aggravation. Before becoming a novelist, Tina, along with her sister, joined their father's pool supply business, knowing their father owed money to suppliers and years of back taxes. The outcome for each sister was markedly different. "My sister is a happy-go-lucky, conflict-free gal, and she can deal with our father," explains Tina. "My sister accepts the tax debt and makes sure it gets paid now. She's gotten really good at running the business and has taken over."

Tina, on the other hand, didn't last a year; she found working in the office an absolute nightmare—partly because people were calling, asking to have their bills paid, and her father refused to take any of the calls. "What I have are just bad memories. I admire my sister for being so accepting in the face of Dad's belief that rules don't apply to him. I wasn't able to do that," says Tina.

If you can arrange to test the water of a parent-daughter or parent-son business union, you may be able to save heartache, disillusionment, and disappointment. A predetermined trial period allows both of you to see if you work well together and if you can keep your personal relationship separate. Akiko was trained in theater set design in college; her father had established himself on Broadway, owned a small set design company, and hoped Akiko would work alongside him. Akiko tried. "I interned with him after college, and he gave me advice about my work. He wasn't very helpful because he had certain ideas about how things should be—he was rigid. He had a pretty high opinion of himself, and I didn't think I could do things his way. We disagreed too often, but rather than argue, I slowly moved away from set design. Within a year, I branched off into costume design and moved to L.A. to work in motion pictures."

Given an attraction to your parent's business and the right temperamental match, however, you can work well together. Barbara's father was totally resistant to her coming into his business, but she hounded him until he relented and gave her a division of his bottling company to run. They found out they had a lot in common beyond their love for each other. Once he saw she could handle the business, his perception of her changed, and he didn't feel as if he had to control every detail anymore. "He sits back and lets me do it," says Barbara. "I talk to him three times a week to update him on my division, and he's thrilled that we share the business and that I've had babies. He got a business partner he trusts and became a grandfather. We both got what we wanted."

POINTERS ON JOINING THE FAMILY BUSINESS

- Carve out your own niche.
- Ask for what you want.
- Give disagreements time to diffuse.
- Respect a parent's experience.
- Separate your work life from your personal tie to your parent.
- Compromise to preserve your personal relationship.
- Don't sacrifice your relationship with a parent over business differences.
- Consider your options: If it's not working or you're unhappy, move on.
- Suggest to a parent that the timing is not right for you to join the business (or to return to it).

Measuring Up

Whether you choose the same occupation as a parent, join the family business, follow a parent's hope for you, or go off in your own direction, parents' expectations flavor the tenor of the relationship and how you feel about yourself. Jade has a "nonstop" working mother who is a big go-getter in sales. When Jade thought about reducing her own workload from full time to part-time to start her family, she panicked, not about the reduced income, but about how she would respect herself and what her mother would think. "All I've ever known," she says, "is pressure and working and being on the run like my mother. Hers are big shoes to fill, and I can't do it."

Parents who constantly "raise the bar" with each of your achievements make it hard to be pleased with your own accomplishments. Even if you're a high achiever, you can feel as if you never measure up. Kathrine's parents set stiff standards for their daughter, and no matter how well she does, they tack on a bigger goal. They never seem satisfied. "'I would be so proud of you if you did such and such' is my father's line. You want your parents to be happy with whatever you're offering them," laments thirty-one-year-old Kathrine, a motivational speaker and group leader. "A lot of times, I don't want to tell him when good things happen because they won't be important enough. I tried to talk to him about his expectations for me, but he's oblivious. I decided it's my issue, not his. I need to deal with his hopes better instead of trying to make him see things my way."

Your job successes and failures are closely linked to your and your parents' attitudes toward money and the questions money raise: Are you able to support yourself and your family? Do you have a future in whatever field you choose? Is the status of the job important to you or to your parents? Are you happy? Are they pleased? Your and your parent's answers often don't jibe, and when you define success differently, both of you have many more issues with which to contend.

Fred is less inclined to build a secure future and ignores his parents' practicality. What worries and irritates Fred's parents seems not to faze Fred. Fred, thirty-five and single, has yet to hold what most consider a regular job with paid vacations, medical coverage, and other benefits. He bounces around from job to job, and prefers short-term service jobs. His parents worry that he's not putting any money away for retirement; they wish he would swallow the bitter pill and get a full-time job with benefits. "It wouldn't be worth it to me. I couldn't take forty hours a week, every week, not liking what I do," argues Fred, who has an undergraduate degree in landscape architecture. "I prefer to pick up a plumbing job here, a paint job there, lay a foundation. I won't be absorbed by the system, and it makes my parents anxious. Their biggest fear is that I can do strenuous physical labor now, but what will I be doing when I'm fifty-five?"

Many parents cannot accept that their adult children are responsible for themselves—that who they are and what they become no longer reflects on them as parents. Tony, thirty-one, believes his father blames himself and his divorce from Tony's mother for his son's lack of motivation and job direction. Tony failed a grade in high school when his parents got divorced and did horribly for the rest of school, dropping out of college and getting involved with drugs. As he was from a middle-class family, with two parents who attended college, Tony was expected to finish college. His father was from a very poor family and no one else in it went to college, but he worked his way through paying his own bills. He became a very successful businessman, eventually franchising exercise facilities. "It's hard for my dad to understand how you can screw up your life, first with drugs and then financially," says Tony. "I have a nine-to-five job and am making ends meet, but it's not what my father had in mind for me."

Whatever your parents' point of reference, this is your life, and as in so many areas of your relationship with them, you have to have confidence in yourself and your choices.

Surpassing a Parent

You probably started your career in a better economy with more opportunities for quick success than your parents had, making dollar comparisons unrealistic. Nonetheless, your parents' feelings about your accomplishments and resulting status can breed mixed feelings and real conflict, or conversely a great sense of pride.

The parents of James McGreevey, governor of New Jersey, speak in interviews of how proud they are and were of their son, referring back to his acceptance into Columbia Law School. Rather than being intimidated by the wide gap in their and their son's education and fame, these parents—a nurse and Marine Corps drill instructor—brag about how far their son has surpassed them. You may hesitate to boast or even report success to your parents, however, particularly if you exceeded your parents early on in your work life.

Starting with his first job out of college, Judd earned more money than his father. Judd's earning power makes him "feel edgy and strange. It's not really a problem," he notes, "but I never say a word about how much money I make, because I went to college and my father didn't."

For parents who are less educated than their children, college and graduate school educations can be threatening. Richard says his parents are very defensive and have an unusual position, but it's one your parents may have without expressing it so fiercely. "Our education frightened my parents. Neither of them went beyond high school, and they blame everything they think is wrong with us on college. For us, college opened new horizons, but for them college exposed us to weird, wacko, radical ideas like participating in protests. The fact that all of us went to college is not a point they are proud of. My mother is more proud of the fact that she's raised six tax-paying citizens without a hatchet murderer among us. I don't consider myself more successful than my father. He probably has more money than I do, but my salary is obviously more."

You may earn more or have a lifestyle your parents never dreamed of. Given our money-oriented culture, your income, if vastly different from your parents and/or how you were raised, can cause friction. Jocelyn and her husband are well-to-do by today's standards. They live in a fancy suburb, drive status cars, and travel a lot. Jocelyn's mother is jealous and makes sarcastic comments about Jocelyn's wealth. "When we were about to move to a better neighborhood, my mother said, 'You're going to move to that community and become a snob.' When I got a new fur coat, she said, 'I had to wait twenty years, and mine's so drab.'

"My parents think my husband has a superior attitude because he and his family have money. They've gotten better as we've been married longer. My mother has seen that Greg is a wonderful husband and father. When she starts, I remind her that she always told me to marry up, and that I just followed her advice. And I love reminding her that she's the one who arranged our first date. But mostly I reassure her that I haven't forgotten where I come from."

Wherever you end up on the career scale, how you got there can often be traced back to your parent's guidance and role modeling. Adult children often forget to give their parents credit for the values and traits they instilled that allow their offspring to thrive. When you think about your achievements in terms of parental contribution, you may have a renewed appreciation for their input. Although Stephanie's father has not had a financially productive life, he has given his daughter the tools to accomplish what he didn't. "The drive, the kind of toughness you need to succeed today in business, are the good qualities I got from my father. I translated his work ethic into a lift-me-up type of drive that allowed me to make far more money and be able to help my parents out when they need it."

You can't be everything your parents want and do what you want to do with your own life. Reaching satisfactory work visions for yourself as well as meeting parents' expectations becomes a balancing act. You want to have free rein over your choices, recognition for your successes, and alternately advice and no advice from your parents. As in other areas of your life, acknowledge your parents' hopes and dreams, but gently remind them final decisions are yours. You can accept their disappointment when you separate career decisions and realize that how you earn a living is only one aspect of your relationship and history together. Keeping parents informed of career moves and your on-the-job progress eases their minds and acknowledges the role they played in your future. Give it time. They may modify their strong feelings when they see that you are fulfilled.

TAKING CHARGE OF YOUR OWN CAREER DECISIONS

- Clarify distinctions between your and your parents' definition of success.
- Acknowledge specific input, attitudes, and help they provide.
- Patiently explain your job and what you do.
- Weigh in your parents' aspirations before you react.
- Share your success if your parents are not overly sensitive to it.
- Ask for advice when you think a parent can help, but be vigilant so you are not overly influenced.
- Consider the years of experience a parent has before you dismiss his or her observations or contributions.
- Figure out what may be behind your parents' strong career choice for you—her success or failure in a field; wanting more for you than for himself; wanting you to be independent when she may not have been.
- Be calm, persistent, and rational about your goals.
- Thank parents for making your career options and work life possible.

TEN

Relationship Shifts

The chances are that if you are over thirty, you have experienced at least one sorrowful revision in your life, be it your own divorce or separation or your parents'; the loss of a job; or the serious illness or death of someone close to you. These experiences deeply touch your own life, but also affect your relationship with your parents.

The adult child-parent relationship must be flexible in responding to changes. Any major upheaval or small ripple casts a new spin on interactions. A problem or situation requiring change might come out of nowhere or be known well in advance. For instance, selling your childhood home usually would be categorized as planned, but an illness or death is more likely to be unexpected. Even anticipated changes threaten to rock a steady boat.

As you and your parents move through transitional periods, you'll reevaluate. When you act and react without giving up your independence, transitions should be smoother for everyone. As with your other adult child-parent problems, retain what works and eliminate what doesn't.

People adapt in different ways when there are few pleasing or practical options. What may seem an absurd accommodation to you is a tolerable adjustment for someone else. After their parents' divorce, the siblings in Lillian's family assumed different approaches to their parents. Lillian's sister divides her time evenly between her two parents; Lillian's brother chooses not to see either parent for now; and Lillian feels obliged to visit her mother because she is alone and her father has remarried. "I pretty much do what I feel like in spacing my visits with my mother," Lillian says. In most adult child-parent transitions the system gets jostled, but the new system may give you and your parent a better understanding of each other and bring you closer emotionally.

Illness Changes the Relationship

For most people, the hardest adjustments are those related to a serious illness or a death. Yet those transitions offer a chance to grow and to grasp the importance of your parents and the interactions you have with them while they are healthy. Kim recognized the fragility of life and the value of maintaining the happy relationship she has with her parents when her grandmother died last year. Kim knew her grandmother loved her, but her grandmother had never said the words to her until right before she died. When Kim told her mother about the conversation, her mother picked up on the significance immediately. "Now my mother says 'I love you' every time she hangs up the phone, knowing she doesn't want to be the way my grandmother was. My grandmother's death makes me afraid of losing my parents," Kim admits. "I want to spend as much time as I can with them, and let my son have as much time with his grandparents as he can."

Invariably, there will be an alteration in how the principal parties function together if you become ill—you or your parents or both of you may change. Mya's diagnosis of MS about a year ago strengthened her relationship with her parents. The spotlight had always been on her mother, but this time her mother was supportive. "She has come through in terms of what my expectations are for a mother," says Mya. "In the past she would turn the situation around to focus on herself."

After an adult child's health crisis, once-self-indulgent parents might grow up; irresponsible parents might become more reliable. Roberta saw a significant change in her mother after Roberta was told she had lymphoma. Prior to that announcement, says Roberta, thirty-six, "My mother could be over the top, unpredictable with her emotions. She was so dramatic that we were all held hostage by her in a weird way. My illness forced her to grow up. She stopped the theatrics of losing her temper and slamming out of the house."

Mya's illness also changed her and how she looks at her parents. About the time she confronted her multiple sclerosis, a few of Mya's friends' parents died. Watching her friends cope with their loss changed her attitude toward her parents; she realized that her parents "are not perfect, but they're alive, and I'm lucky. I had two really good friends whose dads died within one year of each other. One had a great relationship with her dad; the other had a terrible relationship with her dad. If you have a good relationship with your parents and they die, it's very sad, but their deaths are not magnified by unresolved negatives between you."

Heidi talks about her mother's bout with breast cancer and her own need to face her mother's mortality and get beyond her mother's obstinacy, a trait that has been a problem for Heidi most of her life. "I see her physical frailties now and am more tolerant of who she is, in that I'm able to be warmer. I call much more often."

When faced with a parent's illness, you may become protective, more worried, and certainly more aware that your parent might die. But the most prevalent outcome of a serious illness, if it is survived, is renewed closeness. When Wyatt was a child, his father was a taskmaster with a violent temper; when Wyatt was thirty-eight, his father suffered a heart attack and had bypass surgery. "Those events were life-changing for him," says Wyatt, forty. "He has mellowed and we are closer than we were. I was afraid of him when I was young so our relationship is a lot healthier now."

Life-threatening illness can rattle the foundation of your relationship with your parents and, as Dennis found out, carry with it a new perspective. When his father was fifty-nine, his cancer that had long been in remission flared up and it looked as if he might die. Dennis's father lay in a hospital bed for weeks with his ex-wife and children at his side. Dennis, thirty-one, was still angry with his parents about their divorce, which was finalized when he was nine years old, but spending so much time together in the hospital gave him a better understanding of his parents as people rather than as parents. "My perceptions of them have changed, and I am more accepting of their peculiarities, of which they have many," he says, and smiles.

The jolt of your parent's illness can also cause you to rethink the relationship, especially if it has been a difficult one, and make some drastic changes. From the time she was twenty until her mid-thirties, Glenda, forty-five, was mostly estranged from her parents. Glenda believes "my parents screwed me up and then they couldn't cope with me. They never called to ask me how I was doing. When my mother was told she had systemic lupus, my husband and I were about to relocate to Alaska. I couldn't leave, and not moving was painful because we had been planning and working toward the move for years."

Glenda thought her mother was going to die and began visiting more often and for longer periods of time, eventually moving back to her home state. Like Glenda, you may decide to spend more time with your parents when an illness or death jars your relationship. And, you may find that in helping to care for your ill parent, you become closer to your healthy one.

When a Parent Dies

Most of us think about parents dying abstractly or fleetingly until their serious illness stares us in the face. The death of your parent is one of the most difficult of transitions, and getting through it automatically restructures your relationship with your surviving parent. As Abigail says, "It took a few years after my mother died for me to realize I could talk to my father about my relationships, physical ailments, and pretty personal stuff. I like to think that my relationship with him is the one I would have had with my mother at this point. At this age and stage, most daughters are friends with their mothers."

Madeline's father, who had not been involved in his children's lives or household details, stepped in to assume his wife's position as head of the family after she died. He shocked everyone by sending birthday cards and showing up just to visit. Madeline, thirty-six, previously uncomfortable talking to her father, forced herself to be open with him and allowed him to baby-sit for his grandchildren. Madeline's natural inclination had been to take over for her mother, but she stepped aside to let her father be the family nurturer who, like her mother, offers calming advice and solves family problems in his new role.

Conversely, the death of one parent may necessitate your pulling away from your surviving parent if he or she behaves poorly long after an extended adjustment period. Reducing your contact with a parent after the other parent's death is a form of self-protection that you have the right to exercise. The death of Kenneth's father only widened the gap he felt with his mother. "When my father was alive, he was a pretty good buffer for my mother," explains Kenneth. "She was reasonably pleasant around him. He would keep things going and keep things light, rein her in if necessary. When he died, she became worse, and without him I saw her more clearly. We experimented spending holidays without my mother and decided we like hanging out with just the five of us—me, my wife, and the children. We celebrate being with each other without her. We love it. Everybody's relaxed."

Adult children and parents find themselves instituting changes and switching roles as they work through the transitions accompanying the prolonged illness or death of a parent. You probably won't have to take as severe a position as the one Kenneth adopted, but you are very likely to find yourself assuming a more authoritative point of view.

Losing Your Childhood Home

You or your parents may agonize over the decision of whether to sell the home you grew up in. Blake's mother has lived in the family house for the ten years after his father's death, even though he keeps advising her to buy a smaller house. "The house is too big and too old and consequently too much for her to care for. She spends her time and money having workers rebuild this and that." Blake, thirty-five, understands that "she's being sentimental, and I'm being practical."

Practicality has little to do with the emotions tied up in a home, especially the one where parents raised their family. When parents consider selling the house and relocating, they wrestle with the options of where, what they can afford, and distance from their children and grandchildren. As Zoe, forty-two, pushed for her parents to move to a warm climate and less expensive area than where they are now, her parents stood firm. "They developed this mantra of three statements that they repeated over and over until I backed off: 'You children are what we're around for; we don't want to be away from you; having the grandchildren visit a couple times a year isn't enough for us.' Their staying here makes no financial sense." Zoe grudgingly gave up the battle.

You may be the one who is attached to your childhood home. When your parent remarries and the new partner makes dramatic remodeling changes to the house, you might feel ousted, uncomfortable, or unwelcome. Minor renovations or selling the place you called home can have the same effect. Elaine's father, who is in his early seventies, has remarried three times since being married to her mother, but he has remained in the same house. To Elaine, forty, it's not the same house because the wives have made so many structural and decorative changes it's hard for Elaine to remember what it looked like when she was a child. Her father's current wife has young children, roughly the ages of Elaine's children, so her old room isn't available for her or her children when they visit from out of state. Even so, her father has room for them, but Elaine doesn't feel good about staying there. Instead she makes visits with her father short, and she and the children stay with her mother or other relatives.

Twelve years into her mother's remarriage, feelings remain strained between Nicole and her second stepfather. She felt neither comfortable with him living in her childhood home, nor good about him selling it. Nicole adds, "He moved into the house that was the last house we lived in as a family with my first stepfather, whom I consider my dad. He lived there for the first eight years they were married. When my mother sold the house, I got a box of my stuff and felt very displaced. Now when I visit, it's *their* house."

You may feel more threatened by separation than by the physical loss of your childhood home. Such feelings are common when the family has always been a tight unit, yet some feel liberated by the changes. "After my father died," Courtney explains, "my mother and sisters and I became joined at the hip. Everybody enjoyed the closeness, except me. I felt like there was no room for individuality or breathing." Courtney wasn't unhappy when her mother remarried, sold their house, and planned to move from Dallas to Colorado, but her sister Susan had a terrible time. Courtney, who stayed in Dallas, thought the distance between them would be freeing; Susan, who was relocating at the same time to New York with her husband, feared she was going to be both physically and emotionally removed. To maintain their bond, the sisters and mother speak to each other once a day.

Transitions, be they deliberate or unexpected, can transform a relationship that's been deadlocked for years and bring you and your parents closer. You may have to play a new role, becoming an adviser or a shoulder to cry on. Whatever relationship shifts you go through with your parents, be prepared for difficult periods, but also be open to the opportunity to enhance your adult child-parent connection.

As You Deal with Transitions . . .

- Leave room for forgiveness.
- Be available to listen.
- Discuss options as realistically as possible.
- Offer constructive, concrete suggestions.
- Accommodate a parent when you can.
- Smooth the way if possible.
- Put yourself in your parent's position, so you can be more understanding.

ELEVEN

It's a Boy!

Parents as Grandparents

You have given them the grandchildren they've patiently (or not so patiently) been awaiting. Having
grandchildren is one of life's most thrilling and anticipated
events. But they also produce unanticipated changes in
your adult child-parent relationship. Most adult children,
particularly women, agree that the bond with their mothers becomes closer, yet sometimes what you envisioned in
your relationships with both parents doesn't materialize,
at least not in ways you expect.

For your parents, having grandchildren means acknowledging that they are getting older, which is not such
an easy transition. While grandparents adapt to their new
role, you are dealing with your own new self-image as a
parent and the numerous responsibilities and pressures of
parenting. Becoming a parent also brings a certain loss of
privacy with the invasion of grandparents. For someone
like Diane, who grew up without grandparents, having her
parents visit three times a week unannounced was a
shock. "They live a few miles away," Diane says, "and their

omnipresence began to madden me. They walked in, ignored me, and started talking to the baby. It took a while for all of us to adjust."

The arrival of a baby moves you from your central position in your parents' world, a shift that can be surprising, as Nicole found out. She noticed a profound difference in her bond with her mother. When Nicole was pregnant, her mother went overboard buying her maternity clothes and hovering. When baby Charlotte was born, Nicole's mother stayed for two weeks while grandmother and grandbaby bonded. "I felt Charlotte replaced me, and later the same thing happened with my son," Nicole remembers. "Even now, when my mother and I are together and I ask her a question, she doesn't answer, she's totally absorbed by the kids. We haven't had time for each other alone, not more than an hour's worth of face-to-face conversation, in seven years." Nicole, an only child, lost her premier status in her mother's heart to her children. Despite her previous cravings for less attention and more independence, she is not pleased with the change.

Until you become a parent, it's hard to fully appreciate your parents and the sacrifices they made to raise you. Mya confesses, "My mother has an extraordinary gift for taking care of children. Watching her interact with my children, I am amazed by her creativity and natural ability and have a new appreciation for what she did, raising the four of us.

"My father," Mya says on a lighter note, "buys clothing for the kids. He takes great pleasure in walking into a store and choosing outfits that I'm not embarrassed for them to be seen in. He has impeccable taste. It's a side of him I never knew and would not have seen unless I had had children."

Caring for your own baby can also bring to light things you didn't notice or took for granted about your parents when you were growing up. Amanda finds her father's time commitments to his children admirable now. He put his children before his work, and what he sacrificed became evident as Amanda, twenty-eight, transitioned to being a parent. "Dad was the chaperone for a one-week trip with my seventh-grade class. It occurs to me that he had to use a week of his vacation time to do this. I never questioned that my dad would be there whenever I needed a ride or was sick."

Your having children usually has a profound effect on your parents as well, and may be the change they need to truly acknowledge your passage to adulthood. With the arrival of her son, now a toddler, Kim, thirty, and her parents were able to move successfully and smoothly into a relationship as adult friends "which is probably why we are so close," Kim points out. "The parentlike interaction is with my son, not me. We are all intent on introducing Bradley to new experiences and take him to museums, shows, the beach, together. I feel like everybody—my mother, my father, my husband, and my son—is happy together. As an adult, I love our relationship."

However, you cannot count on the arrival of grandchildren changing your parents' personality or lifestyle. It's unlikely that your child will turn your mother into a nurturing grandparent if that's not what she's been all her life. Grandparenting, however, gives your parents the opportunity to make amends for their inadequacy as parents and to experience "parenting" in a new way.

Baby-boomer grandparents understandably arrive at grandparenting from a different place than their own parents did. Most still work, some in high-pressure jobs, and given our mobile society, live great distances from their adult children. You may have to dismiss the idea of your parents bike riding and baking cookies with your children on Friday afternoons or visiting on weekends on a regular basis. Retirement comes later for many, prohibiting their spending a lot of time with grandchildren.

Ignoring the way things are, you may still latch onto ideals: parents who entertain your children, regale them with stories, and treat them to an assortment of memory-building delights as if they lived around the corner. You may envision your parents sharing family lore and enriching their grandchild-grandparent bond. Or you may dream your parents will arrive with chicken soup at the first sign of a sniffle, yours or your child's. Some grandparents deliver, but some don't.

Not Living Up to Your Expectations

If you had engaging, attentive grandparents, you'll probably expect the same from your parents, and any deviation will be upsetting. Your parents may live in another state or be too busy to be like the grandparents you grew up with. They may be less involved than your own grandparents were. That doesn't mean they love your children any less.

Youth-obsessed parents may not gracefully accept the arrival of grandchildren who are reminders that they are getting older. Jessica's mother wasn't ready or happy to be a grandmother. The first of her friends to become a grandmother, she told her daughter she didn't want to be called Grandma. On the other hand, Jessica's mother-in-law was eager to bask in the emotional high of becoming a grandparent and wanted to help whenever she could. "When I got pregnant the second time," Jessica says, "mother couldn't be happy for me, then, either. All she could say was, 'I can't handle you having another baby.' It's all about her getting older, not about me or my happiness. I can't turn to her, but then I never could."

When you have a baby, many of the same problems you had before with your parents resurface. Kenneth acknowledges no change in his mother since the birth of his children, but he wasn't expecting more than he got. "My mother feigns tremendous interest in my children and says how much she misses them, but you put her with them, and all she talks about is herself. She doesn't engage with them on any meaningful level. The world exists to support her and reflect her, as it always has."

Lisa had a similar problem. When her children were young, she hoped her parents would provide much-needed breaks, but they assumed no active role in their grandchildren's lives. They didn't want the responsibility of two children, and they didn't know how to play with them. "It's supposed to be fun to enjoy your kids with your parents, but mine weren't interested," says Lisa. "They would like to see them in a play, but if the conditions aren't perfect, they don't want to attend. They're not easygoing; if it's too hot or too cold, they won't do something like watch a soccer game. My children have to fit into their routine rather than my parents fitting into theirs. They're not flexible enough for grandparenting. I don't know why this surprises me; my parents were always programmed."

When you go against what your parents had planned for you in the way of childbearing, your faintest hopes may be dashed, particularly if you have parents who rarely supported you in other aspects of your life. At thirty-three, Olivia reevaluated her life and decided not to wait for the man of her dreams to have a child. When she was pregnant, her parents wanted her to have an abortion. "I would have loved my family to rally around me, to say, 'You've decided to have this baby; let's do it.'" says Olivia. "I was very angry and hurt that my dad did not back me throughout my pregnancy. When I had Ashley he came to the hospital with a camera to take the requisite photos because he thought he should; he didn't come because he wanted to be there."

Before you confront your parents with your anger, think about the relationship you want your child to have with them. There are some things that don't need to be said or rehashed. Olivia wants Ashley to know her grandparents. Her mother visits with her partner to see her granddaughter once or twice a year, and Olivia doesn't want or expect any more from her. Olivia's father lives in the same town, so Ashley spends a lot of time with her grandfather. "If Ashley's need for grandparents were not so important to me, I would cut loose; I'd never talk to them again. I decided long ago that I have this precious, awesome little girl. I win—no matter what role my parents choose as grandparents," concludes Olivia.

Most distressing are grandparents who choose to be uninvolved because they cannot accept a grandchild's difference or disability. Sasha adopted Kyle when he was four months old and gave up her career two years later when he was diagnosed with autism. "My parents think I should return him, as if he were a Cuisinart that didn't work properly. I don't mind being tied down, not seeing friends, and devoting my life to my son. I'm thrilled when he achieves the smallest goal," says Sasha.

Try to educate your parents to your child's condition, behavior, or need for medications. Give your parent's time to come to terms with the situation. But after hearing, "He'll outgrow it," or similar insensitive messages that indicate grandparents don't understand, you may tire of having your heart broken and choose to distance yourself from your parents, visiting less often and keeping those visits brief.

EXPECTATION GUIDE

- Keep lines of communication open so poor connections can improve.
- Consider your parents' other commitments when evaluating their grandparenting zeal or lack thereof.
- Factor in parents' personalities and distance in their relationship with their grandchildren.
- Be thankful for the positives grandparents add to your family.
- Use in-laws, other relatives, and friends to fill the voids left by your parents.
- Whatever your feelings, protect grandparents' image by speaking favorably about them in front of your children.
- Watch for changes in your parents, which often come with the arrival of and adjustment to grandchildren.
- Don't expect more for your children than you received as a child from your parents; however, you may be pleasantly surprised.

Expectations Met

Grandparenting is an opportunity many parents seize as a chance to fill real or imagined parenting failures or deficiencies. Grandchildren offer a second chance at parenting, to redo a maternal or paternal role from which they were absent or felt lacking the first time around. Sarah's parents divorced before she and her brother started school, so her father never had an opportunity to have a close relationship with his children because he wasn't in the house. "My father is *completely* devoted to the kids," Sarah enthuses. "We see him almost every weekend. My son is his best friend. There's something very nice about that, and something very sad, too. I see him relating in a different way than he did to me. He's gentler as he's gotten older, and he's a lot wiser, but then with his grandchildren, he's not the one being asked to change diapers."

Kim's father, a baby-boomer parent with a long workday and a long commute, left in the morning before his children woke up and didn't return until late evening most days. Like large numbers of fathers of his generation, he didn't have time to do fun things with his children. When Kim got married, seeing her parents every couple of months was fine. After her son was born, visits became more frequent. "Bradley's existence brings us closer because he's so in love with my parents, and my father's absolutely so in love with my son. The happiness I feel watching them together can't be put into words. Every stage is a little different. We're all closer because of my father's relationship with my child."

As your parents interact with their grandchildren, you may discover new facets of your parents' personalities, perhaps because the time together is more focused or because your parents are less stressed. Or maybe you are paying closer attention and seeing your parents from a different perspective. Austin was raised by a very hands-on, stay-at-home mother. When he watched her interacting with her grandson, his appreciation for his childhood jumped to a higher level. Like all parents, she got frustrated with her children's adolescences, but was patient and easy to talk to. "When I saw her with my nephew, her first grandson, I recognized the kind of wonderful environment we had as children, what she did with and for us," notes Austin. "She was reading to Dylan when he was one month old. She's so good with him. He's only four years old, and he can read and write—my mother helped him achieve that. She has an intensely encouraging personality. I see that now."

Inevitable In-Law Comparisons and Conflicts

For all the joy grandchildren bring, they can also reveal your parents' insecurities, competitiveness, and jealousies when they have to share grandchildren with "the other side" of the family. You too have the challenge of seeing the differences and shortcomings in your own parents as grandparents compared to your in-laws. However dangerous, some comparisons are inevitable.

Whether your parents are dream-come-true grandparents or troublesome or unavailable, they can surely elicit resentment and guilt feelings in you when you prefer an in-law for the task at hand. After the birth of her daughter, Elizabeth turned to her mother-in-law, who took charge in what Elizabeth considered a helpful, supportive way. "Being a first-time mother, I was very nervous; my mother-in-law was so much better than my mother, who was not confident. That shocked me. I felt guilty because my mother-in-law was somebody I could talk to if I had a question or a situation I couldn't handle. My mother didn't seem like she knew what to do, which was not reassuring. I wish she felt more comfortable. It's as if she did not have four children; it was difficult for me to reconcile her fears."

Disappointment in your parents can escalate when you have two sets of grandparents with their own unique styles and approaches to your children. Katie and her in-laws live in the same neighborhood, so they have easy access to her children. Her mother-in-law took care of her children for several years after Katie returned to work. Katie's parents live far away and desire the bond their daughter and grandchildren have with the in-laws. When Katie's parents come to visit, the children gravitate to the grandparents they know well. Katie's mother and father want to have their own special time with the children, but sometimes that's not possible because her husband believes his parents can spend time with the children whenever they want. "When my parents are around, it's very stressful for me," says Katie. "I know my parents feel they are being cheated. And they are."

You may feel cheated, too, when your parents don't see your children growing up. Sporadic visits don't compensate for missed milestones or having your parents in the stands at Little League games to cheer on their grandchildren. You can ease long-distance grandparents' feelings of being slighted, as well as the regret you yourself feel, by keeping grandparents apprised of what the children are doing. Offer regular updates of children's new interests and achievements. Keep a picture of grandparents in a prominent place in your house or in your child's room. Talk to the children about their grandparents, have the children telephone, or establish their own E-mail or instant message connection with grandparents. These small gestures prevent grandparents and children from feeling like strangers when they see each other.

Around holidays and birthdays, be sure to tell grandparents what the children would like, so they don't inadvertently select something a grandchild doesn't want or has. When your parents visit, be sure they have ample time alone with their grandchildren to talk, play, and get to know each other better. And when children are young, explain in advance to your parents that the kids may go to the other grandparents only because they are used to being with them. This is something grandparents understand, but hearing it lets them know that you are concerned about their feelings.

Comparisons and tensions peak when family events and holidays force you to choose between parents. One

---

SOLUTIONS TO HOLIDAY DEMANDS

- Caution: Children are easily overstimulated by the holiday rush.
- Remember, children feel (and act on) their parents' stress.
- Devise a plan and inform all grandparents.
- Consider changing a tradition to make your life easier.
- Choose the weekend or a day before or after a holiday to celebrate with parents or in-laws.
- Alternate holidays with family sides.
- Take breaks with young children from family even when visiting.

---

side feels shortchanged, but precise plans need to be made, and you need to enforce the plans *you* make to protect your marriage and children. Each spouse should be responsible for relaying the specifics to his or her parents. This principle should be in effect for visits as well as when time-sharing is a conflict. For example, Katie's parents should be given time alone with their grandchildren during the holidays and their infrequent visits. Everyone wants time, and wants that time to be relaxed, comforting, and special. It can't be if weekends or holidays are a tug-of-war between competing grandparents.

Grandparents who want to spend a lot of time with their grandchildren eat into your time alone with your children. Paige came to dread Saturday, the day her in-laws used to arrive at eleven in the morning to see the baby and stay until after dinner. If her husband was not around, as he often wasn't at least for part of the visit, Paige felt as if she was baby-sitting everyone. She finally told her in-laws they had to come in the afternoon. For the last few months they've been arriving around three o'clock, and her mother-in-law heads straight to the kitchen and starts cooking an elaborate dinner.

"We can order out, but she thinks cooking is her entrée, her pass to see the baby," says this forty-four-year-old mother. "By the time she's finished, it's Renee's bedtime, but my mother-in-law hasn't seen her. She's been too busy in the kitchen. She then insists on keeping the baby up to play with her, and you know what that does to a baby's schedule. My husband needs to tell them they can't be here every Saturday, and I need to start dropping by their house during the week to free up our weekends."

GUARDING YOUR TIME REDUCES PRESSURE

- Explain that you need time alone with your children and partner—and guard that time.
- Settle on visiting arrangements that fit your and your children's schedules and that will not be disruptive.
- Divide available time fairly between grandparents whenever possible.
- Ask grandparents to be amenable to change—and less time—as grandchildren have more commitments.
- Explain arrangements and schedules clearly.
- Be systematic and deliberate in solving time conflicts.

Protecting Your Own

Grandparent involvement often goes way beyond intruding on your time with your partner and children. Grandparents should not interfere with the upbringing of grandchildren, but grandparents on both sides commonly ignore that advice; their interference ranges from how you raise them to how you dress them. Grandparents tend to believe that since they are experienced and you are not, you should heed their advice. They believe their comments and actions are in their grandchildren's best interest, even when you feel otherwise.

If the relationship between you and your parent has been one of close scrutiny, you hope your own children will be the long-awaited diversion. Unhappily, you may find the intense inspection moves to your parenting skills, or lack thereof, from your parents' perspectives. In attempts to make their opinions and feelings known, grandparents manage to be smothering, meddlesome, belittling, or too take-charge. And you are called on to protect not only yourself, but also your growing family.

Her mother regularly rattles Nicole's confidence as a parent. If one of the children is sick, her mother calls and wants to know what the problem is and what the doctor said. "Literally, if she knows I'm going to the doctor, she calls before we get back," Nicole complains. "It's as if I were the nanny and she were the mother. She wants a full report: what the child's temperature is, and she tells me when to take it again—what medicine the doctor prescribed, and when I will give it next.

"She used to ask me what we were wearing, and if I had dressed the children warmly enough. It's awkward when your own mother implies that you're not competent. I see her questions as a form of control, just more of the same, more of what I grew up with."

Here are some things to say or do when your parents

- interfere in ways that feel like criticism: "I know you would prefer we did this your way, but we prefer to learn from our mistakes."
- ask too many questions: "All those questions make me feel as if you're judging me."
- are not being helpful: "It's great that you want to do _____, but what I really need is _____. Can you do it? That would save me so much time."
- want to visit at inconvenient times: "I really want to see you, and so do the children. _____ time isn't good for us, we'll be too distracted. How is _____ for you? We would be able to spend more time with you."

- tell you what to do: "It hurts my feelings and makes me think I can't do anything right; it makes me doubt my own judgment."
- turn small issues into big ones: "We're both upset. Let's talk about it. Tell me your thoughts, we can find a compromise."
- try to outshine one another: Be mindful of the good qualities each one has and keep comparisons to the minimum. Focus on what each offers his grandchildren and promote and encourage those ways of connecting.

Many parents are quick to insinuate themselves into your children's lives if given the room, and some are inclined to blame you when grandchildren don't do well in school, when they get hurt on the soccer field, or when they don't get enough sleep. Anything your parents don't approve of or agree with is portrayed as your fault. If you have an extremely domineering parent, for instance, you will want to limit her contact with the children. Kenneth doesn't permit his mother to impose her beliefs on his family. "My mother makes proclamations about my children that I can't and won't abide. When our son was born, she announced, 'I will not have Catholic grandchildren.' I don't recall giving her the authority to make that decision. She's very verbal about religion, as she is about most things having to do with my children. I give my children the opportunity to be with her, but we keep it very brief, a lunch or dinner, and we stay away as much as possible."

In-laws, it turns out, may not be much kinder or any more understanding than your own parents—and just as dogmatic. In-laws who originally worried about and criticized your care of their son or daughter now second-guess the care you provide their grandchildren. Lucy is at odds with her mother-in-law, who is proficient at undermining her. The tension and dislike create palpable discomfort for Lucy's daughter Hannah, who regularly winds up in the middle. When Lucy tells Hannah she can't have a toy, her mother-in-law buys it; when Lucy says no more cookies, her mother-in-law sneaks one to her. If Lucy tells Hannah it's bedtime, Grandma argues for her to stay up. No matter what position Lucy takes, her mother-in-law takes the opposite. "Our differences are of such proportion, I want to keep my daughter away from her to hurt her, and that's not good. My husband realizes she's impossible, but he also knows she won't change. He just watches quietly and does nothing."

Emma would love to keep her in-laws away from her children but her husband allows his parents free rein with them and does nothing to support his wife—a source of increasing friction between them. Because no limits have ever been set for Emma's in-laws, they come and go and do as they please with the children. This has created an untenable situation for Emma—one that calls for professional counseling to help the couple regain control of their family. "My in-laws have no respect for me whatsoever; they ignore my instructions about feeding, napping, and discipline. They do whatever they want, and it's always counter to what I have said. My mother-in-law thinks these children are hers, not mine."

Beyond preserving the marriage and retaining parental rights, other legitimate concerns may give you reservations about leaving grandchildren in their grandparent's care. Your child's special needs or a grandparent's emotional or physical problems may require caution and the enforcement of hard rules. You are the parent: You decide what you want and don't want your parent to do with your children, and what may or may not be safe for them.

Karen and her siblings don't want their mother driving any of the children, so Karen was shocked when her mother bought a car seat for her own car. The grandchildren visit her for dinner every few weeks and sleep over. "She's a bad driver; she gets very distracted and very lost," Karen explains. "Having her drive the children is not safe. I know she's in heaven when she's with them. They paint and do amazing arts and crafts projects. I trust her to be in her house or around her house with them, but not in a car." Karen had to put her foot down and insist that the children would not be allowed to stay over unless her mother promised not to drive them anywhere.

Parents, not grandparents, know best. You know your children better than anyone else. And while enlightened grandparents understand they should mind their own business, the temptation to share their views on parenting is usually too strong to keep them from offering their parenting knowledge and points of view. Flatter them by asking for their advice, and listen to it, but you don't have to follow it. The more you ask, the less likely they are to offer unsolicited hints and bold suggestions. However, the support of having your parents or in-laws ready to rush in to help you—to arrange their schedules to pick up your children after school so you can go to a doctor's appointment or the gym, or to fly in from out of town to free you for a vacation—is something to keep in your mind when their advice seems confining and demeaning.

Grandparents feel a genuine need to connect with their grandchildren. They want to help and to be with you and your children. Grandparents are the first ones on the airplane to be present when the baby is born. Most go to great lengths to be with their sons and daughters and grandchildren on a regular basis and to stay connected. "Even though it's a long-distance relationship," says Samantha, "since the children were born, it's a rare day when we don't talk, and it's a rare month when we don't see my parents. They usually come to us; we go to them less because it's harder to travel with young children."

Having children unquestionably remolds your adult child-parent tie, and if you make adjustments that let your parents be with your children, you can expect to be richly rewarded. Grandparents make memories that grandchil-

---

Exercising Your Parental Rights

- Don't forget, you and your spouse are your children's principal role models.
- You control grandparents' access to your children.
- Exercise your parental rights to protect your marriage and your children.
- Put your children and spouse first.
- Make and spell out "do and don't" rules for your children and ask grandparents to follow them.
- Remind grandparents calmly that you are left to undo the problems they create.
- Limit time together if visits with grandparents are too stressful for you or your children.
- Ask for and insist on support from your spouse in maintaining sensible parameters with parents or seek professional help.

dren will cherish forever, and they add another cog of emotional security to young lives. The grandparent-grand-child bond is important for carrying on family traditions and rituals, for helping your children understand who they are and where they came from.

TWELVE

Parent to Peer—
The Friendship Model

Benjamin, a fifty-two-year-old marine biologist, re-members a day some twenty-five years ago when his father called him to relate his dream from the night before. "'You and I are riding in the back seat of a car. You turn to me and say, 'I need to borrow your pants.' I'm wearing gray slacks, blue blazer. I take my pants off and give them to you. You put them on, and in spite of the difference in our size, they fit. I feel very good about that.'

"I believe it was at that point my dad recognized I was functioning independently and had achieved the level he assumed for me: I was out in the world, a professional. It was no longer that I was less and my father was more; we were from that point on fairly equal grounds. He has treated me that way ever since."

Unlike Benjamin's father, whose dream was a kind of epiphany, parents can have difficulty recognizing that their offspring are adults with whom they could be friends. Peter wishes that he and his parents "could enjoy each other as mature adults, as parent and child, *and* as friends. But what we pretty much have is parent-child, with an occasional breakthrough that seems more like friendship. That's just the way it is. I can't make my parents something they're not."

Of course you can't force your parents to change, but with gentle guidance and a friendship model to follow, you can help your parent become a peer—a gratifying progression indeed. As with any other friendship, your new relationship with your parents may be a passing, casual friendship or a warm, intimate one, with all of the attendant pluses a best friend offers.

People become friends for different reasons, and rarely does one friend meet all of a person's needs—one may be a confidant, while another is both a running buddy and an expert sports conversationalist with no interest whatsoever in your private life. Even with your closest friends, you filter out certain things you don't want them to know. Leslie, forty-two, sees the distinction with her parents. "Most of the time I tell my mother everything going on in my life, but then sometimes I don't. I wish I had a sister. I don't want to tell my mother things I tell my close friend or would tell a sister. Telling my mother aspects of my private life is very uncomfortable for me."

Cara practices intelligent protectiveness in withholding information from her mother, a wise approach if your parent is a chronic worrier. "I probably don't tell my mother everything," Cara states. "I don't tell her the things that are really worrying me because I don't want to worry her."

With friends, you expect personal tastes to be similar because you form the relationships based on compatible interests, personality traits, and mutual experiences. But as we all know well, we don't choose our parents, and our interests, traits, and experiences may not mesh very well.

Even so, it becomes necessary to view your parents as people, acknowledging their strengths and limitations, as most people do with their friends. The elements that go into making and keeping friends are the same ones you can use to transform parents into peers.

FRIENDSHIP'S CORE ELEMENTS

- A shared history
- Common interests
- Concern and caring
- Support and trust
- Mutual respect
- Love and affection
- Forgiveness
- Acceptance
- Respect of privacy
- Ability to listen

Starting Points

Friendship with your parents is likely to be a satisfying relationship if you adhere to the fundamentals and tenets that mark strong friendship. Consider your own healthy friendships in terms of the core elements. After you weigh these elements in relation to your most cherished friends, even those that date back to your childhood, you'll realize those ties are not as close as the ones you have with your parents. They can't be. The comfort and concern levels and shared history are difficult to replicate with a friend, no matter how deep the friendship.

Thea's mother is the kind of friend who shores her up or walks her through the possibilities whenever she's having difficulties. Her mother does it well because, as Thea recognizes, her mother "knows me better than anyone else. She knows things I haven't realized about myself. When I call her with a problem, she has two basic speeches: You work so hard, you've done so much, you put such high expectations on yourself. Then there's the kick-in-the-ass speech: You're the one who wants to do all this, you need to get on your feet and do it. And she usually gets the right one, but if not, I say, Mom, we need the other speech." Those who move parents into the peer category benefit from having a parent/friend who rarely lets them down and who is usually on their side.

As good friends do, Thea's mother comes to her daughter's rescue and bails her out on occasion. "My husband and I were going to a wedding, and I didn't have anything to wear because we live in the South and the wedding was in New York. She went out and bought something that was exactly my style, not her style, and it fit perfectly."

Having grown up with and adopted some of your parent's ideas and ideals also insures a natural starting point for a parent-peer friendship. Josie's dad is a Democratic state senator and Josie, thirty-three, is a lobbyist for AIDS. Their congruent values give them lots to discuss. "We're not like families with staunchly liberal parents whose children turned out Republican," Josie points out. However, differences such as one being a Democrat and the other Republican, one being an atheist, the other devoutly religious, shouldn't negate the friendship. Rather, as with friends, you avoid political, religious, or other touchy discussions.

Adult children who have a history of connection to their parents or whose ideological thinking is similar to their parents' have an easier time implementing the friendship model, but friendships are possible wherever you begin and whatever the jolts along the way. Judd is thirty-two, and when presented with an invitation from his father to spend time together he panicked. They had rarely, if ever, been alone. His mother was going out of town, and his father was looking for something to do on a Saturday afternoon. Judd was terrified at the prospect of spending four or five hours with his father. "We had a very strange relationship; I always felt I was a disappointment to him," confesses Judd. "A lot of it might've been me projecting it onto him, but a lot of it was actual disappointment. The outing was a big turning point in how I relate to my dad. We had such a good time, we've done it five or six times since. It was a long time before I got to like my dad, but it's been really satisfying to me to get to know and appreciate him."

Angela, thirty, and her younger brother, Jake, began a friendship with their father with no grounding other than their blood tie. Their father had disappeared from their lives before Angela's ninth birthday. Their mother remarried and divorced several times, so Angela and Jake practically raised themselves. This year, when Angela's company relocated its headquarters, Angela moved from Kansas City to New Jersey, near their father. Jake, who was job hunting, decided to join his sister. "We never felt as if we had a father and basically had to start over with him," comments Angela. "It's late to begin to know a parent, but Jake and I are so happy that we have the chance. Being with him was strange at first, but Dad's a wonderful guy, and he loves us. We are learning about each other. We have a parent again and a new friend, even though at this point, we don't need much parenting," she says with amusement in her voice.

In contrast, Mya began her adult relationship with her father from a strong position, as she sees it: "Our relationship has developed into this incredible friendship over the years. Once the curfews and rules were gone, miraculously the relationship changed. Dad became the kindest, most sincere, loyal friend I have. I can call him up and pretty much tell him anything. I can cry with him, laugh with him; I'm able to be totally open with him. I used to hide all that from him when I was a teenager. He's supportive of everything I've done in my life."

Eight Ground Rules for Ensuring Friendship

As with peer friendships, adult children and parents have to make an effort to have a fulfilling friendship. Even people who have intensely troublesome relationships with their parents can forge an improved, more friendlike relationship by playing a leading role in what should start to feel like an equitable collaboration. Here are some simple ground rules for becoming and remaining supportive, loving allies.

GROUND RULE 1: LET GO OF "OLD STUFF"
Old wounds and issues—the emotional leftovers from childhood—inhibit developing friendships. In order to have a sincere friendship with your parents, you have to let go of stuff that happened years ago. You may have to forgive your parents for being human and try to forget the errors

they made or you think they made when you were growing up. Some mistakes parents made were due to not knowing any better or being under terrible strain. Often once the pressure of supporting and raising a family has been lifted, people change. Even when they don't, consider that when a friend upsets or hurts you, if you value the friendship, you forgive that person or at least tuck the incident away to preserve what you have together.

Richard adds unaffectionate and unsupportive to the long list of his descriptions of his parents, yet he is able to get beyond the many tribulations he experienced as a child. "I still remember when I saw my high school friend kiss his dad good-bye, I was overwhelmed. I said to my-self, 'Look at these people! They actually hug, kiss, and touch each other,'" remarks fifty-year-old Richard, who would have preferred that his parents show affection and anger. In Richard's family, displaying either emotion was viewed as acting illogically. It took him many years to learn it's okay to let someone see that you're upset. "It would have been nice if my parents were different, but they are who they are. I'm an adult. Whatever I grew up with, this is who I am. They raised me; I owe them that much, and I love them."

Similarly, Isabelle remembers her father as a rigid taskmaster. He was hard and demanding; nothing was good enough for him, it had to be better, and if Isabelle did something wrong, she paid the consequences. She couldn't get away with anything with her father, and pun-ishments were severe, but Isabelle vows to work around his deficiencies. "That's the past," she says. "I try to think about what I got from my father's rigorous upbringing and his focused life. He knew what he wanted and knew how to get it. He was the same way raising his children, but he taught us to be independent, to have a plan, think through the plan, and to have a backup plan. I appreciate having those abilities and store the unhappy parts of my childhood only to remind me what not to do with my own children. That frees me to have a different kind of relationship with my father. My parents retired recently, and my father is learning to enjoy himself and have fun. I would like to be part of his more relaxed life."

At times it's much easier to fault parents for your unhappiness or failings than to admit to yourself that you made mistakes or are accountable for your own behaviors and disappointments. Rebecca, a thirty-three-year-old mother of three, used to blame her parents for her unfinished college education. Rebecca wanted to go to school out of state, but attended a small local college because her parents said they didn't have the money for her to live away from home. Rebecca believed they didn't trust her, and to rebel she dropped out of college, an action for which she took no responsibility. Later, when she claimed she would have her degree if her parents had let her go away, her husband encouraged her to admit that she could have stayed in school or gone back if getting a degree had been important to her. "You have to get over that," he told her, for the sake of her present relationship with her parents.

GROUND RULE 2: ADDRESS NEW HURTS PROMPTLY

As you strive to make relationships with your parents more like those with peers, new hurts or glaring affronts may arise. Small rebuffs, such as a parent's insensitive comment about a meal you prepared, forgetting your spouse's birthday, or preferring a round of golf to a visit with you, can create rifts in the relationship; but like the larger ones, they can be surmounted. When new offenses occur, explain to your parents how their behavior has upset you. Then be prepared to forgive them and let go of your resentment.

For Mercy, a divorced thirty-seven-year-old photographer in New Orleans, it was hard to forgive her parents for not coming to the hospital after she was sexually assaulted. They live an hour's drive away; when the emergency room called to notify them that their daughter was being treated, the nurse told them it wasn't necessary for them to come.

"When they've had problems, minor ones, I'm there in a flash without a second thought; I don't call and ask people what I should do," Mercy says. "On top of being in pain, with my body violated, I'd never been hospitalized. I was utterly crushed by my father and mother's insensitivity and their unwillingness to deal with the rape. I wound up spending the night in the hospital. I was, or maybe it just seemed that way, the only person without a family member with them. I felt a huge barricade slam down in my relationship with my mother and father."

Instead of letting her resentment fester, Mercy called her parents a few days later after she had begun to pull herself together and asked them why they hadn't driven to the hospital. Her mother dismissed their absence by saying she couldn't handle it, but Mercy could think of no acceptable excuse for her father, and she told him so. "I felt if I didn't let them know how I felt, the division between us would just get wider and wider. My father finally admitted that he had made a bad decision, and we've worked through some of the issues surrounding the rape, but we haven't mentioned their absence from the ER since."

GROUND RULE 3: FACE AND WORK
AROUND PARENTS' SHORTCOMINGS

To allow for friendship, it's best to work with the elements of your parents' personalities that you like or love—and work around the ones you don't. Compensate for the flaws as you see them; at this point it is unrealistic to think you can change your parent's approach to life or have your parent face his or her own demons and failings.

Most of us can find faults—some serious—that impede our relationships with our parents, but there are viable ways to deal with parents' shortcomings. You may have a judgmental or argumentative parent with whom you've spent a lifetime in disagreement as Ariel, fifty, has. "The pickings are pretty slim when I look for things to talk about with my mother," comments Ariel. "She has never been interested in what is going on in the world; we have almost no family left alive, and pitiful little to discuss that doesn't escalate into arguments—ones that tend to settle around my daughter's emotional difficulties or my ex-husband. To avoid conflict, I keep our visits centered on movies (she's a movie fanatic) and Scrabble. Those are safe areas we both enjoy. We play Scrabble marathon fashion and don't tire of it. And, of course, there's no end to gossip about movie stars."

Rebecca considers her mother's lack of emotional openness to be a shortcoming. She wishes she and her mother could talk about their feelings and personal problems, but her mother doesn't get close in that way. Rebecca has decided to pay attention to her mother's good qualities and accept the fact that they talk about superficial things, about clothes, store sales, and parties. It isn't the kind of relationship Rebecca wishes it were, but her mother's heart is in the right place. "She's a wonderful, good person," Rebecca says, "and that's what keeps me calling her, and seeing her, and wanting to share my life with her. We're close because I'm the only daughter and I have daughters of my own, not because we confide in each other or share our disappointments."

When you're trying to have a friendship with a controlling parent, you will have to be accepting while staying guarded. At forty-four, Heidi recently discovered how to navigate the rough road she and her mother have been traveling. Having children helped Heidi understand a little more about her mother's craziness and not get caught up in it too often. Her mother is unable to put Heidi's interests or desires first; hers always have a greater priority. Heidi, who wanted validation as an adult and as a parent, was looking forward to having the whole family meet at her house for the holidays. She wanted to sit at the head of the table in her own home at Christmas or Thanksgiving, but her mother patently refused to come to Heidi's house for any holiday. When Heidi realized her mother was a control freak, she dropped the holiday fight.

Heidi is pleased with the progress she's made. "The change really came from me. I started viewing myself differently and acting differently. As a result I engage less in arguments and power struggles with her. I feel less of a need to defend myself or have her approval. I've let go of my own stubbornness so we can be more compatible."

Adult children are usually willing to tolerate more and bend more with a parent than they would with a friend because the relationship with a parent is permanent and far-reaching. Lillian is thirty years old, and although she doesn't depend on her parents, doesn't look up to them, doesn't confide in them or ask them for advice, she wants them in her life. Under these circumstances she has found the only way to do so. Lillian knows, "I'm not going to change a thing about them. My father is controlling and needy; my mother is fearful and socially inept. They will always stress me out. What allows me to have a relationship with them is accepting them for who they are and what they can give."

GROUND RULE 4: ESTABLISH AND GUARD YOUR BOUNDARIES

Your conversations with parents may not differ much from those with friends, but there are times when you need to keep your boundaries sharp, times when it's necessary to draw—or redraw—the line. Thirty-three-year old Tricia discusses most things with her parents, but when the conversation turns to her social life, her restrictions go into effect. Her parents are very interested in her dating life and hope their last child will find her match. "They don't meddle and are not too pushy," Tricia explains, "because I stop them if the questions get too personal. They want more information than I want to share. I don't give my best friend private details, so I'm certainly not going to tell my parents."

Parental inquisitiveness throws the balance of respect off-kilter, but a parent's candidness also may be a definite breach of boundaries. Mercy and her father developed camaraderie soon after Mercy graduated from high school, and any topic was fair game between them. Of her father, says Mercy, "When I was younger I thought, my God, we're so close, he told me this and this. There are a lot of things I wish he didn't tell me. A daughter doesn't need to know the intimate details of her father's sex life."

Even when limits are respected on both sides, you can

have difficulty sticking to the rules you have put into place. If you are a person who relies heavily or are dependent on your parents, be particularly careful to adhere to the guidelines you set for yourself and the relationship. Samantha, thirty-two, admits that she has no self-restraint when it comes to keeping anything from her parents. "I tell myself that I'm an adult and I don't have to share everything with my parents, but that thought lasts about ninety seconds before I pick up the phone. I hide nothing from them, good and bad. My mother calls it 'processing,' although she has told me several times I don't *need* to vent as much as I do to her, that I have a husband who will listen," Samantha says. When you tell too much or more than you mean to, you leave room for a parent to step in and control your life, and often your thinking—precisely what boundaries are designed to prevent.

GROUND RULE 5: STAY CONNECTED

When kept within the established boundaries and not excessive, communication is the most powerful tool for sustaining friendship. Those who share information regularly keep the bond alive. E-mail access has transformed many relationships, allowing them to flourish across great distances. Beyond the ability to transfer news instantaneously, you can share photos and motion pictures of family-related events, even your baby's first minute of life, with a click of a mouse.

Jennifer's parents have used E-mail for over ten years and own a digital video camera. Her dad is a retired aerospace engineer, so the family grew up using computers and video cameras. Jennifer, a journalist and known gadget freak, gave her parents a digital picture frame last Christmas so they could swap photos. The system downloads digital pictures via cable lines at her parents' home in New Mexico. She lives in England and can't imagine keeping in touch without technology.

You may, however, find the telephone and E-mail more than sufficient to prevent your relationships from waning or going stale. Adult children, particularly daughters, acknowledge speaking with a parent two and three or more times a day about things that range from important to trivial. Roberta, who lives in a different state than her parents do, combines E-mail and telephone to keep their friendship central. She says, "Hearing my mother's voice is more satisfying to me than E-mail."

GROUND RULE 6: INITIATE CHANGE

You can be affectionate to parents who were always cold; you can speak up to parents who did not permit you to voice opinions when you were young; you can announce when your feelings are hurt or your parent is being inconsiderate. Growing up, many children did not have these privileges, any one of which puts you on a more equal playing field with your parents. The ball has moved into your court.

Because of his stiffness, Isabelle's father is unable to show real emotion and affection. "A big hug would feel better to me than his saying, 'I'm proud of you.' I'm going to start throwing my arms around him. Maybe he'll learn from me," Isabelle hopes.

When Elizabeth was a child, she was afraid to argue with her opinionated father. As an adult she challenges him face-to-face when he's being unreasonable. "The communication is more open, I feel I can tell him when he says or does something that upsets me," Elizabeth says.

When Elizabeth's parents visited her brother and sister-in-law and their newborn, her father complained that the baby kept him up all week. She knows he has little patience, but his nonstop complaints got Elizabeth wondering if her ten-month-old daughter bothers him when her parents visit her. She asked him outright if Frannie annoys him, too. Confronting him made him realize he was adding stress to already stressful situations, and he stopped complaining. He apologized to his family and made sure they knew that he wanted to be with his grandchildren, screamers that they are. "He can survive a few nights of interrupted sleep," adds Elizabeth.

By verbalizing her concern directly, Elizabeth addressed her father's insensitivity, and he heard her. Now the family can be together without worrying that he's unhappy.

Elizabeth's frankness improved their relationship, but some parents are incapable of accommodating their adult children's needs. They can't be more flexible, affectionate, communicative of their thoughts, or do whatever you see as the antidote for your relationship. To establish and retain a friendship with these parents, you have to focus on ground rules 3, 7, and 8.

GROUND RULE 7: DISCOVER AND SHARE MUTUAL INTERESTS

Friendship is less demanding when the people involved have interests that draw them together. For some adult children and their parents, one joint interest is enough to sustain the friendship. In the relaxed atmosphere of whatever you're engaged in, conversation slips into other areas, and you may discover mutual interests or passions to add to the foundation of your relationship.

Peter and his father share an affinity for cars and business. Peter sees the time they spend talking about their favorite topics as a breakthrough, another step toward the friendship he seeks with his father. Recently his father called him at the office and asked if he had any appointments during the day. Peter's schedule was clear until the next day at noon. They jumped in his father's car in downtown Atlanta, and the next thing Peter knew they were in North Carolina. Peter suggested turning back, but his father wanted to go further. They ended up in Washington, D.C. They spent the night, and early the next morning his father dropped him off at the airport and stayed to see the sights.

Peter presents his view of the adventure: "When we drive, when we're in that little capsule, we do a lot of talking, a lot of bonding, and it's nice. When we're in that venue we tend to talk more about business than anything else. I don't pry into his personal life or his past, because he doesn't allow it. I would like to know more, like what really happened between him and my mother, but he chooses not to talk about it—it's his business. I respect his privacy."

When a friend is reluctant to talk, a good friend controls his curiosity, holds the probing questions. Your parent's history, especially if there has been a divorce, may be too painful to discuss with you. You don't necessarily have to have deep, meaningful conversations to feel aligned with a parent in the same ways you feel connected to a friend with whom you fish, play ball, or quilt. With certain friends, the activity itself is the connection, and it can be so with parents who shy away from personal conversation.

Gardening, music, shopping, collecting, and sports are among the pursuits that bring together friends, parents, and children alike. Gardening became one of the strongest connections between Los Angeles acupuncturist Nina, thirty-seven, and her mother, even though Nina hated gardening as a young girl when her mother tried to interest her in it. Over the years they have talked about a lot of things—politics, art, books, diets—but never flowers.

About two years ago Nina discovered gardening on her own and is more addicted to her flower garden than her mother. Today they enjoy their conversations about soil and sun, annoying bugs, and yellowing plant leaves. Nina tends to choose species that were in her mother's garden when she was a child, something they find startling, since they haven't lived in the same city in twenty years. Nina sees the irony in all of this. "My mother's eyes light up, and she stares at me in disbelief as I rattle off complex genus names and recommended growing conditions. I think we're both shocked that I somehow retained some of the information she was spewing forth when it appeared I wasn't listening. 'Osmosis' is the word I use to explain how I became so knowledgeable."

Your parent may have limited interests or live a life that is the antithesis of yours. Lisa, who enjoys the outdoors and an active life, has parents who would rather putter around the house. She has no idea what makes her mother happy, but to secure her friendship with both parents, she's circumvented their differences by honing in on something all three enjoy.

Lisa says, "I get my father involved in doing projects in my house—moving furniture, buying new furniture. Both my parents love to cook, so I try to focus on cooking when we talk or get together. I can't just call up and say, 'How's the weather?' That won't do it."

Common interests support, stabilize, and enrich your friendship with your parents. Marion, thirty-four, was able to strike a mutual and glowing balance with her mother, fifty-four. Their shared interests range from religious commitment and wallpapering to weekly family game nights with Marion's children. "I'm both her mother and her best friend," notes Marion's mother; Marion nods her head quickly to indicate strong agreement. Two years after this conversation, Marion's husband relocated, and the family moved a thousand miles away from Marion's parents. The feelings of loss for both mother and daughter were, as Marion says, "almost unbearable. I lost access to my best friend, and it took me a year to adjust."

OTHER TRANSFORMING LINKS ALONG THE PATH TO FRIENDSHIP

- Bring your parents to your job so they can see where you work and meet your colleagues.
- Introduce your parents to your friends, and include parents in social gatherings when appropriate.
- Tell parents about your favorite author or comedian.
- Go to a restaurant together and experience a cuisine you have never tried before.
- Teach parents a game they have never played.
- Join a book or investment club together.
- Take parents to a concert or local theater.
- Get involved in a community project together.
- Start a new family tradition with the grandchildren.
- Plan a weekend trip with your parents.
- Challenge a parent to a game of tennis, a round of golf, or a hand of gin rummy.
- Go bike riding or for a walk together.
- Coach your parents on using E-mail or surfing the Web.

GROUND RULE 8: ADOPT A
THOUGHTFUL, INCLUSIVE ATTITUDE

Be genuinely concerned about your parents, not simply accommodating toward them. One-sided friendships get tiresome pretty quickly. When friendships of any kind work, each party thinks of the other person and tries to arrive at mutually enjoyable ends, a principle that also applies in parent-peer friendships.

In chapter 8, Sharon and her father had a rift over the sale of a condominium they owned jointly. After the condominium conflict was resolved, she was willing to let go of her own self-absorption and be interested in her father's well being. She gets together with her father when her mother goes away to visit Sharon's aunt. She and her father go out to dinner, go shopping, or tackle a project together. They're both very handy, so they will sand a floor or fix a door at her parents' house. "Sometimes I'll ask him to come fix something at my house," Sharon explains, "not really because I need help, but so we'll have some time together."

When she was growing up, Leslie's father attended her high school swim meets and softball games, but as adults they didn't do a lot together. "I learned golf in part because I wanted to," says forty-two-year-old Leslie, "but more so to tap into my father's passion for the game. He loves golf, and it's always a good time when we're together on the course."

Your interactions don't necessarily have to center on activities. Just keeping your parent at the forefront and offering support will shore up the friendship. Lynn is sure of what makes her friendship with her mother work: "There's a lot of give and take between us. I get advice from her— I use her as my sounding board—and she'll call me about a real estate client she doesn't know how to handle.

"When I have conversations with my mom, I think about her strengths and talk about art, history, and the stock market, because those are topics she's up on and knows about. I'm not going to talk to her about the Grateful Dead or some high-fashion trend. I think, what are her strengths that I can pull out of her?"

If you are thinking about your parents in unselfish ways, and your parents are thinking about you, the friendship will flourish. Above all else, your parent wants to be remembered and included in small but meaningful ways. Little things mean so much in friendships and become increasingly important as your parents age. Gordon, a fifty-year-old San Diego computer specialist, worked out a routine that is both thoughtful and energizing for his seventy-seven-year-old father, who lives in Chicago. Gordon bets on sporting events with his close friend John. They bet only televised games; the bets are small, but the competition between the men is keen enough to keep them glued to their television sets all weekend—be it golf, basketball, football, or baseball season. After "placing his bets" with John, Gordon calls his dad to tell him who he "has" in each game.

"My father groans at some of my picks, cheers others, and proceeds to follow the games as intently as I do. We had talked sports during my youth, so it seems natural to include him," Gordon explains. "He's getting older at this point and knowing the betting choices gives him a way to be active in part of my life.

"Forever my champion, Dad calls after the last game to analyze the results of my day. He says things like, 'You buying dinner, son?' if I've had a good day; or, forever the parent, if things went poorly for me, he jokingly asks if I need to borrow money to pay my debt. For decades my father bet with a friend who has died, so my betting with John in some way keeps him connected in spirit to his friend and in life to me." With very little effort, Gordon has continued a tradition and re-created feelings of companionship for his father.

As friendships mature, traditions and rituals become the underpinnings in parent-peer relationships, helping to secure them. Some traditions let your parents know how vital they are to you; others are just fun. The longer a tradition exists, the more significant it is as part of the friendship. With friends or parents, it might be celebrating each birthday together or taking a yearly trip. "No matter where we are or how old we get," says Charlie, forty-eight, "my brother and I battle clogged telephone lines at midnight on New Year's Eve to call our parents. We know those calls are as important to them as they are to us. They show we care, that we're thinking of them."

The Intangibles That Fortify Friendships

In your adult child-parent friendship, with so many elements and so much history working together, the intangibles are the true binding factors: how sensitive you are to each other, your capacity to listen, and your ability to suspend judgment—the very same traits so treasured in a peer who is your friend. These qualities inspire thoughtfulness, trust, and devotion. It's not only the things you and your parents do together, but also the way you think about and respect each other that prompts people like Cara to say, "She's my parent, but she's also my best friend."

What makes Cara and her mother's relationship so special is in small part what they share, but more so the genuine enjoyment they get from each other. Cara elaborates: "The reason she's my friend is she's very smart, knows a lot about a lot of subjects. We talk on the same intellectual level. We have a similar sense of humor and laugh a lot. She's just fun and very engaging. There's a lot of things my mother and I have in common, and a lot of things we don't."

A friend can't fulfill every need, and even among the best of friends, disagreements arise. This is especially true with your parents. Parents get on your nerves, as can other friends, but that's life. A difference can threaten to dissolve a relationship, but a strong friendship, like the one you have the power to develop with your parent, more often than not survives and becomes stronger and closer.

KEYS TO PRESERVING YOUR PARENT-PEER FRIENDSHIP

- Stay in touch regularly.
- Make your goal one of give and take.
- Be appreciative when parents do something for you.
- Build a sense of camaraderie and inclusion.
- Be thoughtful, sensitive, and supportive.
- Isolate and focus on your parents' positives.
- Work around real or perceived parental shortcomings.
- Respect each other's differences.
- Accept what you can't change, change what you can.
- Don't expect parents to meet all your needs.
- Verbalize your feelings.
- Guard and adjust your boundaries whenever necessary.
- Be open to change; friendships continually evolve.

THIRTEEN

A Work in Progress— The Generational Picture

Whatever the former dynamics of your relationship, your father or mother is no longer tying your shoelaces or signing permission slips for you. In other words, you untied the apron strings long ago. For most adult children, parents' rules and the drive to be the "good child" are a thing of the past. Now the emphasis is on friendship and on the benefits and discoveries that emerge from your new relationship.

Adult children who have their parent-peer connection firmly in place are poised to learn about parents in new ways and to make a crucial and lasting impression on their own offspring. Project to the time your children will be adults. Imagine them, if you can, married, raising your grandchildren. Like your parents, you will want them to be an active and integral part of your life. So it is important to be a good friend to your parents not only for your personal satisfaction and enjoyment, but also for the messages you send to your children about family. Their young eyes are watching and absorbing how you relate to your parents.

From the Same Cloth

Parents are our most influential role models, our most enduring connection. The attachment to parents and the emotional fallout from that bond remains, even if we don't see or speak to them.

Physical family resemblance is one small piece of the family continuum. In a conversation with his mother, James, thirty-two, summed up their resemblance: "I'm you, but in a different generation and different gender."

Some of your best and worst traits come from your parents. "We're of the same cloth," Lucas reflects. "For a long time I've been aware that I picked up a lot of my father's personality in terms of being fairly quiet myself and at times difficult to reach emotionally. And, like my mother, I'm a worrier to the point of being neurotic."

Elizabeth sees "a lot of similarities between my parents and myself, more than I care to admit. I noticed more of them after having a child of my own, particularly in how I deal with her. Those are the best ones."

Emily finds the passage of familial tendencies amusing. "My mother is becoming so like my grandmother, who grew up during the depression. She turned the heat up and down, the hot water on and off, and diluted the ketchup with water to save money. As my mom gets older, she does many similar things. She doesn't have to live so conservatively, but she's always trying. What's scary is, lately I've been telling my children to turn off the lights."

The journey of personality traits and behaviors down generational lines concerns many adult children. They frequently find themselves copying behaviors they dislike in their parents and fear becoming their parents.

Olivia checks her behavior whenever she thinks she acts like her mother, who often screamed and hit Olivia and her sister. "My worst nightmare is being the kind of mother my mother was. When I hear myself sounding like my mother, I go in the bathroom, look in the mirror, and say, 'Mother, is that you?' I take a breath, and remind myself that whatever I'm upset about with my child is not something that will matter in ten years. I don't want Ashley to feel the way I did about my parents. I don't want my daughter to ever be afraid of me as I was of my mother."

"My father takes over when he thinks something is not being done correctly," says Carmen, who quickly admits that "if something is not being done the fastest, most efficient way, I butt in and take over, too. I find that behavior so upsetting in my father, and I'm appalled to see it in me."

Recognizing undesirable personality traits is helpful in suppressing them. Sharon, who is forty-one years old, became aware of the similarities between her father and herself early in her twenties. "I think I have the same control issues that he has because he was so controlled as a child, and I was so controlled by him. My goal is to break the chain. When I was younger, I would say things to people, and I wouldn't mean them in a nasty way, but they would come out too harsh. Once I figured out what I was doing and where it came from, I changed my language and found that I could still get my point across without being a controlling bully."

Rebecca has decided to try to break the cycle of avoiding painful and unhappy issues she had with her mother. "I'm going to do with my daughters what my mother was unable to do with me. I am going to ask them what is wrong when they seem distressed. I'm going to be aware of their difficulties and available to them if they want to talk about their problems."

Being grown up gives you the distance to separate out what you think of as harmful or irksome patterns so you don't transfer them to your children. But even with steadfast determination not to duplicate unwanted behaviors, you may find yourself repeating annoying habits as you try to avoid them. Elizabeth, reluctant to talk about those parental traits she wishes she didn't have, notes how her mother's sweetness and lack of self-confidence have crept into her own behavior. "My mother often tends to say and do things to avoid conflict instead of standing up for her beliefs. I sometimes see this in me and am trying to be more assertive and less of a pushover."

When asked about his father, Wyatt laughs at his own observation: "He has a terrible temper, but as I get older, I get more and more like him, so maybe I shouldn't criticize him for that."

The imprint of parents is too great for you to be totally successful at removing every disturbing parental trait. Amy, the mother of two young children, divulges that she fails terribly: "What I don't like in my dad is what I don't like in myself."

Parents Are People, Too

It's best to accept the fact that the perfect parent doesn't exist. All parents make mistakes; mistakes are part of the parenting terrain. Most parents have at least one personality trait or parenting pattern their adult children don't like, want, or value, one that has left an indelible mark on them.

Yet the adult children I interviewed almost universally came to the same realization: "My parents did the best they could. Even if it wasn't great, they tried, and that goes a long way in my forgiving them."

Adult children discovered that the most basic insights into their parents altered the tenor of the relationship and left room for friendships to develop, especially when they recognized that parents are human, with flaws as well as virtues, like everyone else. This new perspective freed them to become more of a friend to their parents:

- "I realized my mother is just a person, not the super-power she presented herself to be—what I saw as a child and even as a young adult in my twenties. She has faults, even though I don't want to accept them. I see her as just a person who tries her best. I'm changing my high expectations of her, because I see she can't meet them." (Courtney, thirty-one)
- "A few years ago it dawned on me that my parents were once fourteen, they had to go through adolescence and grow up, too." (Monica, thirty-four)
- "The most interesting thing I discovered about my parents is they are human; what I mean is, they really enjoy each other, are really in love, and know how to live life to the fullest. They didn't seem like that when they were raising us; they were grumpy and overstressed." (Isabelle, thirty-one)
- "I learn more about my parents as people now that they don't 'parent' as much." (Sharon, forty-one)

Insights like these allow you to know your parents as people, to share their lives as grown-ups. When you look beyond the parenting role, you find new things to enjoy about your parents. Spontaneity worked for Sheri, thirty-nine, and her father. They went off for a week together driving through the northwestern United States with no plan. If a town seemed interesting, they explored it. They hiked and talked. "I heard about my father's childhood, which made me see why he's so family-oriented, why he's such a kind person. It was just great."

When Karen's parents visit, they prepare elaborate meals together, something there was no time to do during Karen's childhood. "When they leave," comments Karen, "I'm completely invigorated and feel so healthy that I am inspired to cook more for my husband and sons." Her enthusiasm for her parents and what they do together filters down to her children.

By accepting and relating to your parents as people, you can learn fascinating things about them. "My mother, it turns out, wasn't as angelically innocent as I had believed. And I now know that even though my dad was the loud one and is difficult to talk to, he is actually quite fragile and emotional. I've been able to see his caring, vulnerable side," Carmen explains.

You may unearth a parent who is different, sometimes weaker, sometimes stronger, sometimes more relaxed and more fun to be with. You may uncover surprising skills and admirable traits—a tenderness that may have been buried under layers of emotional or financial parenting stress.

Ten years ago Eileen viewed her relationship with her parents much differently than she does at thirty-seven. "I see our relationship as both dynamic and evolving. Ten years ago I only saw my parents in black-and-white terms, but they don't feel static anymore. My relationship with my father, which was not good because of his drinking and the divorce from my mother, keeps getting warmer and more positive."

In short, you'll discover more reasons to love your parents. There's no telling what new piece of history or well-kept secret will be revealed to explain something about your parents, about the family, and ultimately about you and your link.

And the Bond Goes On . . .

Statistically, people are living longer and staying healthy longer, potentially giving you the opportunity to reap the rewards of your markedly improved relationship for many years. But don't become falsely complacent. No one can predict how many years you and your parents will have.

When Inge's mother was diagnosed with breast cancer, Inge faced the possibility of losing her and took the experience as a wake-up call. When her mother regained her energy, Inge reevaluated her thinking and now spends as much time as she can with her parents. "Fortunately, my parents are young enough of mind and relatively healthy, so we don't seem so far apart in age, and we can do things together. My father still beats *me* on the tennis court. I consider my friendship with them a very positive part of my adult life."

There has been no medical wake-up call in Elizabeth's family, but she maintains her friendship with her parents because they have a history of friendship and support. "After my husband, I call my parents with any kind of news. My parents have been my best friends since college," the thirty-year-old mother of one says. "They don't judge me, and they help me whenever I ask. I feel comfortable and secure with them. They instilled a confidence you didn't always get from other places. It's nice to be with people when there's no effort required. I can be fully myself and not worry about someone judging me. If I act irrationally, they're going to love me regardless. It's the kind of relationship I want my daughter to see."

Modeling for the Next Generation

Even if you are discouraged, keep trying to improve your relationship with your parents and draw closer to them.

Alexia's relationship with her mother had been nonexistent for so many years, and she had a poor relationship with her father for most of her adult life. When she announced her engagement, her father had a lukewarm response, and she felt "betrayed and hurt. I have had to learn what to expect from my father, and that's not much." Alexia refused to give up on the relationship. "Two years later I called to tell my father I was pregnant and prepared myself for any reaction. To my amazement, his utter joy and excitement were genuine. It's late, but it's a beginning for us." Alexia was motivated to continue working on a positive and healthy relationship with her father for herself and for the sake of her child.

Emily is at the other end of the vast adult child-parent spectrum, having had an exemplary relationship with her parents. Like most adult children, Emily takes issue with her parents in a few areas, but feels they were predominantly loving and supportive. "My parents are wonderful people. I appreciate them very much; they're giving and loving. That's the environment I grew up in. I admire their selflessness: they put their children before themselves,

---

CREATING A SUCCESSFUL MODEL

- Stop harboring grudges and nursing injustices for things past.
- Look for more ways to love and enjoy your parents as people, as well as parents.
- Be patient and persistent in seeking rewarding routes to a parent-peer friendship.
- Watch for changes in parents or in you that open doors to new experiences.
- Ask your parents questions about themselves and your family's history.
- Don't be afraid to show emotion and express your feelings.
- Be aware—the model you create with your parents is the one your children are most likely to adopt with you.

---

everything was for their kids. They were very devoted and affectionate with us."

Your relationship with your parents probably falls somewhere between Alexia and Emily, but many adult children with children of their own wonder how they can replicate the parent-child friendship with their children.

Amy styles her parenting on the kind she received. "I owe a lot to my parents and am very conscious of the fact that I got to be who I am because of them," she begins. "When my sister and I were growing up, they listened to us. Our ideas were valued; they spent a lot of time talking to us. They made us feel important and were and are very demonstrative in showing their emotions. Now that I have children, I respect how they raised us and plan to emulate them as best I can. To be able to say as an adult, 'I love my parents, I enjoy and like my parents,' speaks well for them."

The example you set is part of your legacy to your children. The way you treat your parents, the support you give each other, the fun and experiences you share are the friendship model for adult child and parent relationships that will be passed down the generational line to your own children.

Author's Note

Nobody's Baby Now is based on "grounded theory," a research methodology that in this study interprets the voices, feelings, and perspectives of the adult children who shared the details and progression of their adult child-parent relationships. Grounded theory was developed in the mid-1960s by sociologists Barney Glazer and Anselm Strauss as a means to study social psychological processes; the resulting data is "grounded" in the participants' responses. The "data" consists of participants' stories collected during interviews, then sorted and analyzed. Recurring themes, trends, and patterns unfold and eventually lead to a theory about the group being studied.

Grounded theory was chosen because it works well for topics on which little research exists, because it is highly descriptive, and because it exposes psychological aspects of the adult child-parent relationship that are almost impossible to capture in empirical research. The subjectivity and personal aspects of this family relationship are complex and dynamic; grounded theory allows the relationship to be examined in depth, something other methodologies cannot accomplish as successfully.

The research began with open-ended questions posed to adult children who volunteered from all parts of the country. The only defining characteristics of participants were that they be between the ages of twenty-seven and fifty-five and have at least one parent who was primarily financially and physically independent of their adult child. Because of the randomness of the selection process and the cross-section it represents—some adult child-parent relationships are quite "healthy," some are not—the study provides a realistic overview of the issues, contradictions, and possibilities in adult child-parent pairs.

Participants were assured confidentiality and given pseudonyms. In addition to changing their names, other identifying points such as jobs have been altered in ways that ensure their anonymity, but do not change the accuracy of their socioeconomic levels, nature of their interests, or the types of lives they lead.

One hundred and fifty interviews, most by phone, some in person, lasted between one and one and a half hours and focused on life experiences that would help understand the paths of adult child-parent relationships. After demographic information was collected, the questions were probing and open-ended, differing from traditional interviews in which standardized questions are used. As categories of responses emerged from the initial interviews, questions were added to the subsequent interviews and additional less formal conversations to explore possible links, provide clarification, and assure relevance rather than leave their discovery to chance. Grounded theory is thus controlled by the emerging data; in other words, after the first set of interviews, the research is guided by what the beginning data suggests—in this study, how patterns and circumstances affect adult child-parent relationships.

Grounded theory is not limited to interview material but supplemented by the researcher's observation, previous knowledge, and conversations, all of which enrich the study by providing more than one way of understanding and validating—also called "saturating"—the developing theory. The stories/data are constantly compared and contrasted for similarities and differences. Data collection stops when no new information or themes are being offered and responses become repetitive.

The categories that emerged from this project have been organized into chapters and reflect the issues with which adult children are most concerned. Their personal stories, not raw statistics, reveal and illuminate the very human interactions between adult children and their parents. These stories led to a theory of friendship as well as a guide for developing adult child-parent friendships. The friendship model evolved from the overriding desire among adult children—and conviction—that they should enrich their relationships and become friends with their parents. As with all theory, it is relevant to the group studied and can be modified, as the text suggests, to meet individual needs and circumstances.

Index

Page numbers in italics indicate boxed text.

Acceptance
  of parent(s), 21, 208, 224
  of parent's new partner,
    111–12
  of parents' position, 155
Achievement (adult child), 163
Actions of parents
  understanding reasons
    behind, 40–41
Adjustment periods, 3, 94–95
Adult children, x, xi, 7–9
  treating as baby, 27–29
Advice, parental, 5, 194
  regarding career, 154, 155
Alterations, necessary, 2–4
Anger, 5, 144–45
Annoyance threshold, 26
Annoying behavior (parent),
  27–36
  checklist for managing, 36
Appreciation, expressing, 147
Approval, parental, 22–23, 30
Asking hard questions, 44–45

Asking for help
  from parents, 119–20
  from siblings, 121, 121
Attitude
  in blended families, 109
  modifying, 27
  thoughtful, inclusive,
    215–17
  toward money, 134, 163–64
Attitude change
  adult child, 22, 29–30
  parent, 155

Baby-boomer grandparents,
  180–81, 185
Babying, parental, 27–29
Backgrounds of parents,
  14–17
Behaviors of parents
  copying, 220–22
  modifying, 27
Belief systems, 16
Birthdays, 188

Blending families, 106–11
Bond(s)
    forging stronger, xii
    grandparent-grandchild, 196
    parent-child, 7, 24, 35,
        68–69, 159, 220, 225–26
Bond with mother
    effect of grandchildren on,
        178, 179
Boundaries
    checklist for drawing, 79
    defining, 74–76
    drawing, 71–86, 97
    establishing and guarding,
        208–9
    setting, 85–86

Career(s), 154–68
    expectations regarding,
        156–58
    in family business, 158–62
    surpassing parents in,
        165–68
    taking charge of decisions,
        168
Caring for children, 179–80
Change
    before initiating, 24
    initiating, 18–22, 210–11
Child raising, 12, 91–92
    grandparents' interfering
        with, 190–92
Childhood, ix–x, 17
    leftovers from, 26
    of parents, 14–16
Children of adult children, 43,
        66, 195
    disabled, 183–84
    and distance from parents,
        63
    messages about family, 219
    modeling for, 226–28

relationship with grandpar-
        ents, 104
Choices
    empowering, 22
    in how you interact, 78
    making, 18–22
    in sibling conflict, 124
Committed relationships, 66
Communication, 52, 63–64,
        209–10
Compromise, 94
    minimizing, 2, 3–4
    in religious conflict, 91
    sharing grandchildren with
        in-laws, 186–89
    siblings in, 122, 124
Connection, 8, 9, 53–70,
        209–10
    options for smoother, 61
    reestablishing, 63–65
Control, 7, 27, 33–36, 209
    in money matters, 136–38,
        139, 140–41
    over parent, 24
Controlling parent(s), 20, 207
Conversation(s), stopping, 65
Crisis(es), 23–24, 73
Criticism (parent), 7, 22,
        30–31, 32
Cultural differences, 90–91

Death(s), 169, 170–71
Death of parent, 171, 173–74
    and money, 143–45
Dependency, 73, 77
Devastating circumstances,
        65–66
Disagreement, ix–x, 6
    in friendships, 218
    history of, 39–40
Disappointment in your par-
        ents, 187

Disinterest (parent), 11

Distance, 61–63
  and favoritism, 127–28
  and grandparents, 187–88
  and sibling roles, 120

Distancing yourself from parents, 35, 184

Divorce, 16, 101, 103, 169, 170
  parents' condition after, 104–6

Dynamics of relationship, xi, xii, 129, 219

E-mail, 38, 59, 64, 187, 209, 210

Education, 14, 166

Egocentricity (parent), 89–90

Emotional bond, 2–3

Emotional conflict
  over financial help, 145–47

Emotional dependency, 62

Emotional distance, 108, 120

Emotional needs (parent), 71–72

Emotional problems, 42

Emotional support, 46

Emotional voids, 48, 49

Emotionally dependent parents, 83–86

Emotionally distant parents, 43–44

Emotions, 12–13
  in joining family business, 159
  money and, 137–38
  tied up in a home, 175

Empathy, lack of, 45, 46

Enabling, 126

Estrangement, x
  turning around, 63–66

Expectations about grandparents
  guide to, 184
  met, 184–86
  not living up to, 181–84

Expectations of parents
  regarding career, 163–65

Expressing yourself, 20–21

Familial tendencies, passage of, 220–22

Families, new, 106–11
  seeing differently, 114

Family businesses, 158–62
  pointers on joining, 162
  trial period in, 161

Family fishnet, 9–11

Family obligations, 66–67

Family system, 118–20

Favoritism, 125, 126–29
  understanding, 129

Financial affairs, parental involvement in, 139–41

Financial component in career expectations, 157–58

Financial help
  parents needing, 148–52

Financial help from parents, 123, 136–37, 140–41, 142, 145–48

Financial success, 134–35

Forgiving your parents, 41–42, 202–3

Frequency of contact, 58–61, 62
  and fixing estranged relationship, 64

Friend(s)/friendship, xii–xiii, 4–6, 9, 48, 223, 225–26
  core elements, 199
  eight ground rules for ensuring, 202–17
  emphasis on, 219

intangibles fortifying,
217–18
keys to preserving parent-
peer, *218*
starting points, 199–202
transforming links along
path to, *214*
Friendship model, xii, 197–218

Gay issues, 12, 127
see also Homosexuality
Generational differences,
11–17
regarding money, 133
Generational line, 226–28
Generational picture, 219–28
Generosity of parent, 145–48
coping with and understanding, *148*
Generosity to parents, 149
Goals, parent-child differences,
13–14
Grandparent-grandchild bond,
196
Grandparenting, 180–81, 182
opportunity to fill parenting
failures, 184–85
Grandparents
comparisons with in-laws,
186–89
interference in child raising,
190–92
meeting expectations,
184–86
not living up to your expectations, 181–84
parents as, 178–96
reservations about leaving
children with, 193–94
Ground rules, new, 22
Grudge-holding parent, 64

Guilt, 8, 10, 33, 53
Guilt trips, short-circuiting,
55–58
regarding in-laws, 186–87

Help from parents
money-related, 140–41
sibling needing, 123–24
see also Financial help from
parents
Histories
parent, 11–12, 44, 212
parent/child, xi, 17–18
Holidays, 67
and grandparents, 188–89
parent's new partner and,
112–14
siblings and, 124
solutions to demands of, *188*
Home, childhood
losing, 169, 175–77
Homosexuality, 19–20, 92–94,
122
Hurts, addressing, 204–5

Ideals
adopting parents', 200
in grandparenting, 181
parenting, 142, 143
Illness, 169, 225
changes parent-child relationship, 170–73
Independence, 2–3, 5, 10–11,
16, 74
boundaries and, 73, 76
and relationship gaps, 43
Information
about career moves, 167–68
sharing, 209
withholding, 47–48, 198,
208, 209

In-law relationsip guide, *100*
In-laws, 48, 66–67, 96–100
  and grandchildren, 186–89,
    192–93
  support from, 49–50
Inquisitiveness (parent), 208
Insecurities (parents), 88–89
Insensitivity (parent), 38, 45
Instant messaging, 59, 187–88
Intimacy, parental, 71
Irritants, removing/modifying,
  37–40

Jealousy, 66, 127
Job loss, 169
Job success/failure, 163–65
  see also Career(s)

Keeping everyone happy,
  66–69

Lack of awareness (parent),
  45–46
Lesbianism, 44, 45, 93
Logistics
  with parent's new partner,
    111–14

McGreevy, James, 166
Making your feelings known,
  113–14
Manipulation (parent), 27,
  33–36
Marriage, 87–88
Measuring up, 163–65
Mentors, in-laws as, 49, 50
Mistakes (adult child)
  blaming parents for, 204
Mistakes (parent), 203–4, 222
Model
  creating successful, *227*
Money, 7

attitudes toward, 14,
  163–64, 166–67
claiming rights to parents',
  141–45
earning more than parents,
  166
that obligates, 138–39
receiving from parents, 123,
  136–41, 142, 145–48
Money management, 149–51
Money matters, 133–53
  tips for handling, *153*
Mutual interests, discovering
  and sharing, 211–14

Near or far dilemma, 61–63
Neediness, in sibling, 123

Obligation, 8, 9
  money in, 138–39
  "Old stuff," letting go of,
    202–4
Overcompensation, 15
Overprotectiveness, 15, 27
Oversensitivity (parent), 38–39
  actions to take with, *39*

Parent
  adult child becoming, 178,
    179, 182
Parent-child interaction, 17–18
Parent-to-peer relationships,
  xii, 219
  see also Peers
Parent type(s), xi
Parental rights, 194
  exercising, *195*
Parenting, 11–12, 180, 222,
  223, 227
  abusive, 42–43
  grandparents and, 190–91
  parents' views on, 194

Parenting failures
    grandparenting opportunity
        to fill, 184–85
Parenting ideals
    and money matters, 142,
        143
Parenting role, giving up,
    54–55
Parenting styles, 129
Parenting success
    child's career and, 156
Parenting your parents, xi,
    80–86
    questions to ask, 85
Parents
    aging, 5–6, 181
    changing, 51–52
    driving you crazy, 25–52
    financial self-sufficiency,
        141–42
    as grandparents, 178–96
    involvement in financial
        affairs, 139–41
    living their lives through
        adult children, 71
    needing financial help,
        148–52
    receiving money from,
        136–41 (see also Financial
        help from parents)
    remain parents, 22–24
    surpassing, 165–68
Parents' money, claiming rights
    to, 141–45
Parent's new partner, 7,
    101–16
    barriers to welcoming, 102
    and childhood home,
        175–76
    frankness and honesty
        regarding, 111
    guidelines for accepting, 107

and inheriting money,
    144–45
keeping in perspective, 116
logistics, 111–14
puzzling choices, 102–6
questions to ask yourself,
    105
Partner(s), 48, 66
    and accepting financial help
        from parents, 145–47
    calming approaches to use
        with parents in issues
        regarding, 96
    negative attitudes, 68–69
    parents and, 87–100
    parents' disapproval of,
        89–90
    see also Parent's new partner
Past, parents', 69
    see also Histories
Patterns
    changing, 72, 76–79
    from childhood, 2, 3, 6
    new, 20
Peer friendships, xii
Peer-peer bond, x, xii, 5
Peers
    parents as, ix, 2, 22,
        197–218
People, parents as, 69, 199,
    222–25
Personality (parent), 88–89,
    206
    accepting, 51
    grandchildren and, 185–86
Personality mismatches, 39–40
Personality traits, 36–37
    generational passage,
        220–22
Phone calls, 58, 61, 210
    inconvenient, 56–57
Praise, 22

Pressures, parental, 10–11
Privacy
   in-laws and, 97–98
   loss of, 178–79
Problem areas, 8, 27
Protecting your own interests, 190–96
Proximity, 61–63
   and sibling roles, 120
Push-pull relationship, 71, 73

Racial differences, 90–91
Reconciliation, 64
Rediscovering parents, 2
Rejecting a parent, 35
Relationship with parents, ix–xiii, 3, 4, 5, 6, 7–8, 24
   changed by grandchildren, 178
   changed by illness, 170–73
   changing, 21–22
   commitment to improving, 18
   uniqueness of, 125–26
Relationship gaps
   coping with, 43–51
   protecting, 47–51
   ways to bridge, 47
Relationship shifts, 169–77
Religion, 12, 16, 90–91, 99
   issue in raising children, 91–92
Relocation
   adult child, 48
   parent, 175
Relying on parents, 15–16, 23, 73
Remarriage (parent), 103–4, 175–76
Resemblance, 220
Resentments, 4, 5
   and parent's new partner, 110–11

Responsibility for parents, 120
Retirement, 181
Rituals
   family, 196
   in parent-peer relationships, 217
Role(s)
   adult child, 130
   in family, 118–20
   grandparent, 178
   learning, 14
   parenting, 54–55
   switching, 174
Role(s), new (adult child), 51–52
   guidelines for establishing, 52
   with parent's new partner, 106–11
Role models
   in-laws as, 49
   parents as, 167, 220
Role reversal, 82–83

Safety net, parents as, 73
Same-sex relationships, 92–94
   see also Homosexuality
Saying what's on your mind, 77–78
Scrutiny, intense (parent), 27, 30–32
Separation, 169
   created by distance, 61
   in loss of childhood home, 176–77
Sex, 12, 75–76
Shortcomings of parents
   facing and working around, 206–8
   and sibling support, 131–32
Sibling assistance, 129–32
Sibling complications, 117–32

Sibling frustrations, 120–21
Sibling rivalry, 117, 125–29
Sibling support, 117–32
  maximizing, *131*
Siblings
  forceful encounter(s) with
    troublemaking, 123
  help from, *121*
  high-maintenance, 121–24
  managing problems caused
    by, *125*
  and money, 142
  pitting against one another,
    34
Social differences, 90–91
Social position, 16
Spouse
  and accepting financial help
    from parents, 145–47
  and in-law problems, 98–99
  parents' disapproval of,
    89–90
  parents and, 87–100
  support from, 48, 49
Staying connected, 53–70,
  209–10
Staying in touch, 55, 56
Stepbrothers/-sisters, 108–9
Stepfamilies, 109–10
Stepparents, 109–10
Subconscious ties, 73
Support, 48
  from in-laws, 97–98
  from parent(s), 46, 71
  from spouse, 48, 49

Taking action, 37–40
Temperament, 126, 162
Thinking
  altering, 37, 40–43
Time

guarding, with grandparents,
  189, *190*
Time to spend with parents,
  53–55, 57–58, 66
  loss of, to in-laws, 96, 97
Time together, making more
  comfortable, *70*
Traditions, xii, 196
  and career choice, 155
  in parent-peer relationships,
    217
  parent's new partner and,
    112–14
Transitions, 169, 170, 177
  dealing with, *177*
  death of parent, 173, 174
Trouble spots, addressing,
  36–43
  tools for addressing, 42
Troublemakers, 121–24

Underlying issues
  in acceptance of spouse,
    90–91, 96

Values, 16, 167
  in/and career, 160–61
  congruent, 200–201
  regarding money, 133, 134
Visits
  grandparents, 187, 188, 189
  parent's new partner and,
    113
  weekend, 68
Voids, filling, 47–51

Walking away from situation,
  27, 37
Widows/widowers, 101, 103
Worry (parent), 7, 27, 59
  incessant, 29–30